The Sword of the Spirit

Scripture Key References for
Everyday Prayer

Dolly Busolt

ISBN 979-8-88751-233-4 (paperback)
ISBN 979-8-88751-234-1 (digital)

Copyright © 2023 by Dolly Busolt

All rights reserved. No part of this publication may be reproduced, distributed, or transmitted in any form or by any means, including photocopying, recording, or other electronic or mechanical methods without the prior written permission of the publisher. For permission requests, solicit the publisher via the address below.

Christian Faith Publishing
832 Park Avenue
Meadville, PA 16335
www.christianfaithpublishing.com

All scripture is taken from the Revised Standard Version of The Holy Bible, copyright 1971, New Testament Section. Second Edition. By Division of Christian Education of the National Council of the Churches of Christ in the United States of America.

Printed in the United States of America

Contents

Preface vii
Foreword ix
Introduction xi
How to Pray xiii

Scripture Key References 1
Abiding/Dwelling 1
Accountable (to God, to Commands) 3
Anointing 4
Anxiety 6
Ark of the Covenant 8
Baptism: Water/Spirit 8
Benedictions/Blessings 11
Born Again 15
Comfort 16
Comfort in Mourning 17
Coming of the Lord: End of Age 18
Confirmation/Clarity 24
Confusion 24
Covenant 25
Death/Dying 27
Defilement/Rebellion 28

Devil	32
Discernment	33
Discouragement	34
Divorce	35
Doubt	37
Eating/Drinking	38
Endurance	40
Evil	42
Faith	44
False Doctrine/Teachers	47
Family (Children)	53
Favor	56
Fear	57
Festivals/Observances—Sabbath	59
Forgiveness	60
Gentleness	62
Giants (Rephaim/Anakim/Nephilim)	63
Gifts of Spirit	65
Giving/Tithing	66
God's True Kindred	68
Goodness	72
Grace	73
Groanings/Speaking in Tongues	74
Healing	75
Specific Healing Scriptures	77
Heart	80
Holiness / Personal Conduct	83
Holy Spirit / Spirit of God	87
Hope	91
Idols	91
Intercession	96
Joy	96
Judgment	98

Kindness	102
Lamb's Book of Life	102
Law	104
Leaders of Church / Those in Authority	105
Love	106
Markings in Flesh	109
Marriage	110
Mercy	112
Money	112
Obedience	113
Oppression	114
Overcoming	115
Patience	115
Peace	116
Popular Clichés/Scriptures	118
Power	121
Prayer	123
Protection	125
Provisions	127
Rainbows	131
Renewal of Mind	131
Repentance	132
Rest	133
Resurrection	134
Righteousness	135
Sabbath	137
Salvation	138
Sanctification	140
Seasons/Times	141
Self-Control	143
Sins	144
Speaking (Positive)	147
Standing (Ground)	150

Strength 151
Suffering for Christ / Afflictions / Trials................................153
Thanksgiving 156
Trust 157
War Room Prayers: Nation..157
Watchman..159
Weapons/Warfare 160
Will of God..162
Winds 165
Wisdom 166
Word of God...169
Worship 170

Notes 173

Preface

The desire for compiling this book was due to an intense love of prayer, but specific prayer for certain needs. As I sat through years of teaching, I realized that the Word of God was alive, active, and powerful, and we were taught to pray the Word and speak the Word to be effective and move mountains in our lives. Through years of intercession, I realized just how important the Word was and how specific it is, but I also needed to know just exactly what the Word said about specific needs. That's when I began my searching and listing of scriptures according to those needs we need met.

I also felt that others might benefit by having specific words to pray for their needs, and having a handy reference makes it all easier. At times, I would get phone calls for prayer; either someone was sick or depressed or just needed encouragement. That's when having a journal handy becomes beneficial. I could just turn to a specific scripture and quote it for them, and by speaking the Word, you spoke power into their lives.

Some topics I listed were for general knowledge or curiosity people might have, especially if they were not quite convinced that these even existed, like the scripture references for giants. Some might not believe they existed, but they are referenced in the scriptures.

All scriptures listed are from the Harper Study Bible, Revised Standard Version.

Foreword

In my almost thirty years of full-time ministry, it's been my honor to shepherd people who have a love for Jesus, a love for prayer, and a love for the precious Word of God.

Dolly is one of those people. The consistency of her Christian walk encourages me as a pastor and a preacher, knowing that she's drinking in what the Holy Spirit brings from the pulpit and using it as fuel to intercede for the church and its leadership.

As you study the many topics of the book, you'll feel Dolly's love for prayer and her obvious calling to be an intercessor. My prayer is that everyone who uses this resource would become equally passionate about learning to pray God's Word as a means of powerful intercession.

I see this book as a threefold blessing to the body of Christ.

It's a tool to help maximize the focus of our prayers from a scriptural foundation. Nothing is more powerful than praying the Scripture into life's circumstances and standing on the promises of God's Word rather than the thoughts, opinions, and expectations of man.

It's a template for the intercessor. Intercessors need to know what the Scripture actually says about the things they're interceding for. This resource provides a quick way to get into the mind of God before we go to the place of prayer.

It's a topical resource for the saints. The many topics included here are not only for the intercessor but also for every believer who studies, teaches, and preaches God's Word. I see countless topical sermon starters in this resource that are ready to be used to strengthen the people of God.

The church needs more prayer, more intercession, and more passion for God's Word. I believe this book will inspire those who use it to catch a love for all those things in a deeper and more spiritually productive way.

Enjoy!

Rick Leonardi
Senior Pastor of Full Gospel Center,
Lagrangeville, New York

Introduction

After years of sitting under teachings from a local church pastor about the true Bible and how we belong and relate to God, I truly was changed by His Word and how it related to me and my life going forward. I loved learning more and more about God and how much He really loved us; I couldn't get enough teaching. I started reading not only the Bible, but other reference books and commentaries as well to extend my knowledge of a holy and awesome God. I would keep journals of scriptures for references on how to pray using God's Word. I volunteered continually in all capacities in the church to help and bless people in whatever way God chose—from choir member, Sunday school teacher, greeter, intercessor, and usher.

Sometimes, I was asked to speak at women's groups or seminars about prayer and intercession.

It was when I sang in the choir that I really felt God prompting me to pray for others, to look out at the faces in the congregation and see their needs. It was like He was showing me how to pray and what to pray for each one. I would keep a prayer journal and document my thoughts and what I prayed for. Many times, I was given inspiration to tell others about what God was saying to them through my prayers. There were many confirmations about His words to them, which showed me that as I sought the Lord in prayer, He would reveal what others needed. It made me happy that I was doing something positive and encouraging others.

A few years later, we had a big church celebration and had speakers come from different parts of the country. One called me out and prophesied over me that I was an intercessor for that church and the leadership, which actually confirmed what I was already doing. I didn't quite understand at the time the meaning of all this, but it encouraged me to continue praying for others, which I always loved doing. Eventually, my roles changed in different areas, and circumstances changed, but I have continued to read, study, and research God's Word, which prompted me to write this reference manual, which I felt would be an asset to others, whether you are already praying or just beginning. God's Word truly changed me as I prayed and also changed others as a result of prayers.

> *For the Word of God is living and active, sharper than any two-edged sword, piercing to the division of soul and spirit, of joints and marrow, and discerning the thoughts and intentions of the heart. (Heb. 4:12)*

How to Pray

When we talk to each other, it's communication; when we talk to God, it's prayer.

Purpose of Prayer is to commune with God, have fellowship with Him. He desires we talk to Him.

Petition of Prayer is to bring our requests before Him in a humble manner to intervene for ourselves and others for issues beyond our control, for our needs and desires.

Principles of Prayer are God's principles of prayer that guide us to worship, submit our attitude to Him and His will; to learn forgiveness, which gives us a clear avenue to be forgiven; and to keep the channel open to prayer. It delivers us from any evil intents. In prayer, we envelop His kingdom and power and receive His joy, peace, and love. Our intentions should be to *know* Him, to worship Him first. He takes care of the rest.

Process of Prayer. Enter in to His presence with thanksgiving and praise. Have adoration for God and what He will do on your behalf. Admit we need cleansing from our daily sin, to be pure before Him and forgiven before asking for our requests. Ask specifically about every detail that concerns you. The most truly great effect of prayer is when we present before the Lord His Word. Successful prayer is built on the Word of God—read it, know it, apply the Word, let it operate in our lives. It has power; know how to activate that power, use it effectively for the glory of God. Let God's Word sustain you. Also, be a good listener; listening is part of prayer. God may speak to you in a special way, and you need to be open to hear what He may be telling you. Pray to the Father in the name of Jesus (Matt. 6:9–13).

Using the scripture keys listed in this book can help you to pray for specific needs and pray more effectively.

Scripture Key References

(Alphabetical, by title)

Abiding/Dwelling

One thing have I asked of the Lord, that will I seek after; that I may **dwell** in the house of the Lord all the days of my life. (Ps. 27:4)

He who **dwells** in the shelter of the Most High, who **abides** in the shadow of the Almighty, will say to the Lord, "My refuge and my fortress; my God, in whom I trust." (Ps. 91:1–2)

Behold, how good and pleasant it is when brothers **dwell** in unity! (Ps. 133:1)

They shall return and **dwell** beneath my shadow, they shall flourish as a garden. (Hos. 14:7)

And the Word became flesh and **dwelt** among us, full of grace and truth. (John 1:14)

Do you not believe that I am in the Father and the Father in Me? The words that I say to you I do not speak on My own authority; but the Father who **dwells** in Me does His works. (John 14:10)

Abide in Me, and I in you. As the branch cannot bear fruit by itself, unless it abides in the vine, neither can you, unless you **abide** in Me. I am the vine, you are the branches. He who **abides** in Me, and I in him, he it is that bears much fruit, for apart from Me you can do nothing. If you **abide** in Me, and My words **abide** in you, ask whatever you will, and it shall be done for you. (John 15:4–5, 7)

Do you not know that you are God's temple and that God's spirit **dwells** in you? (1 Cor. 3:16)

So faith, hope, love **abide**, these three. (1 Cor. 13:13)

That Christ may **dwell** in your hearts through faith. (Eph. 3:17)

He yearns jealously over the spirit which He has made to **dwell** in us. (Jam. 4:5)

Let what you heard from the beginning **abide in you**. If what you heard **abides** in you, then you will **abide** in the Son and in the Father. (1 John 2:24)

No one who **abides** in Him sins. (1 John 3:6)

If we love one another, God **abides** in us and His love is perfected in us. (1 John 4:12)

Behold, the **dwelling** of God is with men. He will **dwell** with them and they shall be His people. (Rev. 21:3)

Accountable (to God, to Commands)

You shall be holy; for I the Lord your God am holy. Every one of you shall revere his mother and his father, and you shall keep My Sabbaths: I am the Lord your God. Do not turn to idols or make for yourselves molten gods: I am the Lord your God. You shall not steal, nor deal falsely, nor lie to one another. And you shall not swear by My name falsely, and so profane the name of your God. (Lev. 19:2–4, 11–12)

You shall keep My Sabbaths and reverence My sanctuary. (Lev. 26:2)

So you shall remember and do all My commandments, and be holy to your God. (Num. 15:40)

You shall not add to the word which I command you, nor take from it. (Deut. 4:2)

Know then in your heart that, as a man disciplines his son, the Lord your God disciplines you. (Deut. 8:5)

And He said to him, "You shall love the Lord your God with all your heart, and with all your soul, and with all your mind." (Matt. 22:37)

So each of us shall give **account** of himself to God. (Rom. 14:12)

And before Him no creature is hidden, but all are open and laid bare to the eyes of Him with whom we have to do. (Heb. 4:13)

Anointing

And you shall **anoint** Aaron and his sons, and consecrate them, that they may serve me as priests. (Exod. 30:30)

Then Samuel took a vial of oil and poured it on his head, and kissed him and said, "Has not the Lord **anointed** you to be prince over His people Israel?" (1 Sam. 10:1)

He said to his men, The Lord forbid that I should do this thing to my lord, the Lord's **anointed**, to put forth my hand against him, seeing he is the Lord's **anointed**. (1 Sam. 24:6)

There Zadok the priest took the horn of oil from the tent, and **anointed** Solomon. (1 Kings 1:39)

O Lord God, do not turn away the face of Thy **anointed** one! Remember Thy steadfast love for David Thy servant. (1 Chron. 6:42)

Great triumphs he gives to his king, and shows steadfast love to His **anointed**. (Ps. 18:50)

Thou **anointest** my head with oil, my cup overflows. (Ps. 23:5)

The Spirit of the Lord God is upon me, because the Lord has **anointed** me to bring good tidings to the afflicted; He has sent me to bind up the brokenhearted, to proclaim liberty to the captives, and the opening of the prison to those who are bound; to proclaim the year of the Lord's favor, and the day of vengeance of our God; to comfort all who mourn; to grant to those who mourn in Zion—to give them a garland instead of ashes, the oil of gladness instead of mourning, the mantle of praise instead of a faint spirit. (Isa. 61:1–3)

But when you fast, **anoint** your head and wash your face. (Matt. 6:17)

And they cast out many demons, and **anointed** with oil many that were sick and healed them. (Mark 6:13)

And while He was at Bethany, a woman came with an alabaster flask of ointment of pure nard, very costly, and she broke the flask and poured it over His head. She has **anointed** my body beforehand for burying. (Mark 14:3, 8)

And when the Sabbath was past, Mary Magdalene and Mary the mother of James, and Salome bought spices so that they might go and **anoint** him. (Mark 16:1)

The Spirit of the Lord is upon me, because He has **anointed** me to preach good news to the poor. (Luke 4:18)

Mary took a pound of costly ointment of pure nard and **anointed** the feet of Jesus and wiped His feet with her hair. (John 12:3)

How God **anointed** Jesus of Nazareth with the Holy Spirit and with power; how He went about doing good and healing all that were oppressed by the devil, for God was with Him. (Acts 10:38)

Therefore God, thy God, has **anointed** thee with the oil of gladness beyond thy comrades. (Heb. 1:9)

Is any among you sick? Let him call for the elders of the church, and let them pray over him, **anointing** him with oil in the name of the Lord. (James 5:14)

But you have been **anointed** by the Holy One, and you all know. (1 John 2:20)

Anxiety

You shall not be in dread of them; for the Lord your God is in the midst of you, a great and terrible God. (Deut. 7:21)

Hear, O Israel, you draw near this day to battle against your enemies; let not your heart faint; do not **fear**, or **tremble**, or be in **dread** of them; for the Lord your God is He that goes with you, to fight for you against your enemies, to give you the victory. (Deut. 20:3–4)

Have I not commanded you? Be strong and of good courage; be not **frightened**, neither be **dismayed**; for the Lord your God is with you wherever you go. (Josh. 1:9)

In my **distress** I called upon the Lord; to my God I called. From His temple He heard my voice, and my cry came to His ears. (2 Sam. 22:7)

But Thou, O Lord, art a shield about me, my glory, and the lifter of my head. (Ps. 3:3)

Give ear to my words, O Lord; give heed to my groaning. Hearken to the sound of my cry, my King and my God, for to Thee do I pray. (Ps. 5:1–2)

He makes me lie down in green pastures. He leads me beside still waters; He restores my soul. (Ps. 23:2–3)

In the day of my **trouble** I call on Thee, for Thou dost answer me. (Ps. 86:7)

Anxiety in a man's heart weighs him down, but a good word makes him glad. (Prov. 12:25)

Therefore I tell you, do not be **anxious** about your life, what you shall eat or drink, nor about your body, what you shall put on. And which of you by being anxious can add one cubit to his span of life? Therefore do not be **anxious**, saying, what shall we eat? Or what shall we drink? Or what shall we wear? Therefore, do not be **anxious** about tomorrow, for tomorrow will be anxious for itself. (Matt. 6:25, 27, 31, 34)

I am with you always, to the close of the age. (Matt. 28:20)

I want you to be free from **anxieties**. (1 Cor. 7:32)

Have no **anxiety** about anything, but in everything, by prayer and supplication with thanksgiving, let your requests be made known to God. (Phil. 4:6)

Cast all your **anxieties** on Him, for He cares about you. (1 Pet. 5:7)

Ark of the Covenant

Behind the second curtain stood a tent called the Holy of Holies, having the golden altar of incense and the **ark of the covenant** covered on all sides with gold. (Heb. 9:3–4)

Then God's temple in heaven was opened, and the **ark of His covenant** was seen within His temple. (Rev. 11:19)

Baptism: Water/Spirit

Nay, but by men of strange lips and with an alien tongue the Lord will speak to this people. (Isa. 28:11)

And it shall come to pass afterward, that I will pour out My **spirit** on all flesh. (Joel 2:28)

He will **baptize** you with the Holy Spirit and with fire. (Matt. 3:11)

He who believes and is **baptized** will be saved. (Mark 16:16)

He will **baptize** you with the Holy Spirit and with fire. (Luke 3:16)

How much more will the heavenly Father give the **Holy Spirit** to those who ask Him? (Luke 11:13)

Jesus answered, Truly, truly, I say to you, unless one is **born of water** and the **Spirit**, he cannot enter the kingdom of God. (John 3:5)

It is the **spirit** that gives life, the flesh is of no avail, the words that I have spoken to you are spirit and life. (John 6:63)

He who believes in Me, as the scripture has said, Out of his heart shall flow rivers of living water. Now this He said about the **Spirit**, which those who believed in Him were to receive. (John 7:38–39)

For John baptized with water, but before many days you shall be **baptized** with the **Holy Spirit**. (Acts 1:5)

Repent, and be **baptized** every one of you in the name of Jesus Christ for the forgiveness of your sins; and you shall receive the gift of the **Holy Spirit**. (Acts 2:38)

But when they believed Philip as he preached good news about the kingdom of God and the name of Jesus Christ, they were **baptized**. Then they laid their hands on them and they received the **Holy Spirit**. (Acts 8:12, 17)

While Peter was still saying this, the **Holy Spirit** fell on all who heard the word. And the believers from among the circumcised who came with Peter were amazed, because the gift of the **Holy Spirit** had been poured out even on the Gentiles. For they heard them speaking in tongues and extolling God. (Acts 10:44–46)

And now why do you wait? Rise and be **baptized**, and wash away your sins, calling on His name. (Acts 22:16)

Do you not know that all of us who have been **baptized** into Christ Jesus were **baptized** into His death? We were buried therefore with Him by **baptism** into death, so that as Christ was raised from the dead by the glory of the Father, we too might walk in newness of life. (Rom. 6:3–4)

For by one Spirit we were all **baptized** into one body-Jews or Greeks, slaves or free-and all were made to drink of one **Spirit**. (1 Cor. 12:13)

Thus, tongues are a sign not for believers but for unbelievers. (1 Cor. 14:22)

For as many of you as were **baptized** into Christ have put on Christ. (Gal. 3:27)

And you were buried with Him in **baptism,** in which you were also raised with Him through faith in the working of God, who raised Him from the dead. (Col. 2:12)

Baptism, now saves you, not as a removal of dirt from the body but as an appeal to God for a clear conscience, through the resurrection of Jesus Christ. (1 Pet. 3:21)

Benedictions/Blessings

"The Lord watch between you and me, when we are absent one from the other." (Gen. 31:49)

And the Lord said, "Behold, there is a place by Me where you shall stand upon the rock; and while My glory passes by I will put you in a cleft of the rock, and I will cover you with My hand until I have passed by." (Exod. 33:21–22)

(The Aaronic benediction) The Lord **bless** you and keep you: The Lord make His face to shine upon you, and be gracious to you; the Lord lift up His countenance upon you, and give you peace. (Num. 6:24–26)

(The Shema) "Hear, O Israel: The Lord our God is one Lord; and you shall love the Lord your God with all your heart, and with all your soul, and with all your might." (Deut. 6:4–5)

You shall be **blessed** above all peoples; there shall not be male or female barren among you, or among your cattle. (Deut. 7:14)

Blessed shall you be in the city, and **blessed** shall you be in the ground, and the fruit of your beasts, the increase of your cattle, and the young of your flock. (Deut. 28:3–8)

Choose this day whom you will serve, but as for me and my house, we will serve the Lord. (Josh. 24:15)

Who shall ascend the hill of the Lord? And who shall stand in His holy place? He who has clean hands and a pure heart, who does not lift up his soul to what is false, and does not swear deceitfully. He will receive **blessing** from the Lord, and vindication from the God of his salvation. (Ps. 24:3–5)

The **blessing** of the Lord makes rich, and He adds no sorrow with it. (Prov. 10:22)

A faithful man will abound with **blessings**, but he who hastens to be rich will not go unpunished. (Prov. 28:20)

(Jesus) "The Spirit of the Lord is upon me, because He has anointed me to preach good news to the poor. He has sent me to proclaim release to the captives, and recovering of sight to the blind, to set at liberty those who are oppressed, to proclaim the acceptable year of the Lord." (Luke 4:18–19)

Bless those who persecute you; **bless** and do not curse them. (Rom. 12:14)

Blessed be the God and Father of our Lord Jesus Christ, who has **blessed** us in Christ with every spiritual blessing in the heavenly places. (Eph. 1:3)

When God made a promise to Abraham, since He had no one greater by whom to swear,

He swore by Himself, saying "Surely I will **bless** you and multiply you." (Heb. 6:13–14)

Blessed is the man who endures trial, for when he has stood the test, he will receive the crown of life which God has promised to those who love Him. (James 1:12)

Household Blessings

Now therefore may it please thee to **bless** the house of Thy servant, that it may continue forever before Thee; for Thou, O Lord God, hast spoken, and with Thy **blessing** shall the house of Thy servant be **blessed** forever. (2 Sam. 7:29)

Now therefore may it please Thee to **bless** the house of Thy servant, that it may continue forever before Thee; for what Thou, O Lord, hast **blessed** is **blessed** forever. (1 Chron. 17:27)

For He strengthens the bars of your gates; He **blesses** your sons within you. (Ps. 147:13)

Material Blessings

You shall serve the Lord your God, and I will **bless** your bread and your water. (Exod. 23:25)

Blessed shall be your basket and your kneading-trough. The Lord will command the **blessing** upon you in your barns, and in all that you undertake; and He will **bless** you in the land which the Lord your God gives you. (Deut. 28:5, 8)

May the Lord give you increase, you and your children! May you be **blessed** by the Lord, who made heaven and earth! (Ps. 115:14–15)

And He will give rain for the seed with which you sow the ground and grain, the produce of the ground, which will be rich and plenteous. (Isa. 30:23)

You shall eat in plenty and be satisfied, and praise the name of the Lord your God, who has dealt wondrously with you. (Joel 2:26)

Parental Blessings

Let peoples serve you, and nations bow down to you. Be lord over your brothers, and may our mother's sons bow down to you. Cursed be every one who curses you, and **blessed** be every one who blesses you! (Gen. 27:29)

The God before whom my fathers Abraham and Isaac walked, the God who has led me all my life long to this day, the angel who has redeemed me from all evil, **bless** the lads; and in them let my name be perpetuated, and the name of my fathers Abraham and Isaac; and let them grow into a multitude in the midst of the earth. (Gen. 48:15)

Travel Blessings

Blessed shall you be when you come in, and **blessed** shall you be when you go out. (Deut. 28:6)

For He will give his angels charge of you to guard you in all your ways.
Because he cleaves to me in love, I will deliver him; I will protect him. (Ps. 91:11, 14)

The Lord will keep your going out and your coming in from this time forth and for evermore. (Ps. 121:8)

Now may our God and Father Himself, and our Lord Jesus, direct our way to you; and may the Lord make you increase and abound in love to one another and to all men. (1 Thess. 3:11–13)

Born Again

I will give them a heart to know that I am the Lord; and they shall be My people and I will be their God, for they shall return to Me with their whole heart. (Jer. 24:7)

And I will give them one heart, and put a **new spirit** within them; I will take the stony heart out of their flesh and give them a heart of flesh, that they may walk in My statutes and keep My ordinances and obey them; and they shall be My people, and I will be their God. (Ezek. 11:19–20)

A new heart I will give you, and a **new spirit** I will put within you; and I will take out of your flesh the heart of stone and give you a heart of flesh. (Ezek. 36:26–27)

Jesus answered him, "Truly, truly, I say to you, unless one is **born anew** he cannot see the kingdom of God." Jesus answered, "Truly, truly I say to you, unless one is born of water and the Spirit, he cannot enter the kingdom of God." Do not marvel that I said to you, "You must be **born anew**." (John 3:3, 5, 7)

So must the Son of man be lifted up, that whoever believes in Him may have eternal life. He who believes in the Son has eternal life. (John 3:15, 16, 36)

Truly, truly, I say to you, he who hears My word and believes Him who sent me, has eternal life. (John 5:24)

Truly, truly, I say to you, he who believes has eternal life. (John 6:47)

He saved us, not because of deeds done by us in righteousness, but in virtue of His own mercy, by the washing of regeneration and **renewal** in the Holy Spirit. (Titus 3:5)

Blessed be the God and Father of our Lord Jesus Christ! By His great mercy we have been **born anew** to a living hope through the resurrection of Jesus Christ from the dead. (1 Pet. 1:3)

You have been **born anew**, not of perishable seed but of imperishable, through the living and abiding work of God. (1 Pet. 1:23)

Comfort

The eyes of the Lord are toward the righteous, and His ears toward their cry. (Ps. 34:15)

The Lord is near to the brokenhearted, and saves the crushed in spirit. Many are the afflictions of the righteous; but the Lord delivers him out of them all. (Ps. 34:18–19)

Cast your burden on the Lord, and He will sustain you; He will never permit the righteous to be moved. (Ps. 55:22)

When the cares of my heart are many, Thy consolations cheer my soul. (Ps. 94:19)

As one whom his mother comforts, so I will **comfort** you. (Isa. 66:13)

Blessed be the God and Father of our Lord Jesus Christ, the Father of mercies and God of all **comfort** who **comforts** us in all our affliction, so that we may be able to **comfort** those who are in any affliction, with the comfort with which we ourselves are **comforted** by God. (2 Cor. 1:3, 4)

Now may our Lord Jesus Christ Himself, and God our Father, who loved us and gave us eternal **comfort** and good hope through grace, comfort your hearts and establish them in every good work and word. (2 Thess. 2:16–17)

Comfort in Mourning

He heals the brokenhearted, and binds up their wounds. (Ps. 147:3)

I have seen his ways, but I will heal him; I will lead him and requite him with **comfort**, creating for his mourners the fruit of the lips. (Isa. 57:18)

To grant to those who mourn in Zion-to give them a garland instead of ashes, the oil of gladness instead of mourning, the mantle of praise instead of a faint spirit. (Isa. 61:3)

I will turn their mourning into joy, I will **comfort** them, and give them gladness for sorrow. (Jer. 31:13)

But we would not have you ignorant, brethren, concerning those who are asleep, that you may not grieve as others do who have no hope. For since we believe that Jesus died and rose again, even so, through Jesus, God will bring with Him those who have fallen asleep. (1 Thess. 4:13–14)

Coming of the Lord: End of Age

In that day men will cast forth their idols of silver and their idols of gold, which they made for themselves to worship, to the moles and to the bats, to enter the caverns of the rocks and the clefts of the cliffs, from before the terror of the Lord, and from the glory of His majesty, when He rises to terrify the earth. (Isa. 2:19–21)

In that day the branch of the Lord shall be beautiful and glorious, and the fruit of the land shall be the pride and glory of the survivors of Israel. And he who is left in Zion and remains in Jerusalem will be called holy, everyone who has been recorded for life in Jerusalem, when the Lord shall have washed away the filth of the daughters of Zion and cleansed the bloodstains of Jerusalem from its midst by a spirit of judgment and by a spirit of burning. (Isa. 4:2–4)

Wail, for the day of the Lord is near; as destruction from the Almighty it will come! Behold, the day of the Lord comes, cruel, with wrath and fierce anger, to make the earth a desolation and to destroy its sinners from it. (Isa. 13:6, 9)

At that time shall arise Michael, the great prince who has charge of our people. And there shall be a time of trouble, such as never has been since there was a nation till that time; but at that time your people shall be delivered, every one whose name shall be found written in the book. And many of those who sleep in the dust of the earth shall awake, some to everlasting life, and some to shame and everlasting contempt. And those who are wise shall shine like the brightness of the firmament; and those who turn many to righteousness, like the stars for ever and ever. But you, Daniel, shut up the words, and seal the book, until the time of the end. (Dan. 12:1–4)

I will utterly sweep away everything from the face of the earth, says the Lord. The great day of the Lord is near, near and hastening fast; Neither their silver nor their gold shall be able to deliver them on the day of the wrath of the Lord. In the fire of His jealous wrath, all the earth shall be consumed; for a full, yea, sudden end He will make of all the inhabitants of the earth. (Zeph. 1:2, 14, 18)

The sun shall be turned to darkness, and the moon to blood, before the great and terrible day of the Lord comes. (Joel 2:31)

Then those who feared the Lord spoke with one another; the Lord heeded and heard them, and a book of remembrance was written before Him of those who feared the Lord and thought on His name. They shall be mine, says the Lord of hosts, My special possession on the day when I act, and I will spare them as a man spares his son who serves him. (Mal. 3:16, 17)

The disciples came to Him privately saying, "Tell us, when will this be, and what will be the sign of your coming and of the close of the age?" And this gospel of the kingdom will be preached throughout the whole world, as a testimony to all nations; and then the end will come. Immediately after the tribulation of those days the sun will be darkened, and the moon will not give its light, and the stars will fall from heaven, and the powers of the heavens will be shaken; then will appear the sign of the Son of man in heaven, and then all the tribes of the earth will mourn, and they will see the Son of man coming on the clouds of heaven with power and great glory. (Matt. 24:3, 14, 29–30)

But of that day and hour no one knows, not even the angels of heaven, nor the Son, but the Father only. As were the days of Noah, so will be the coming of the Son of man, and they did not know until the flood came and swept them all away, so will be the coming of the Son of man. (Matt. 24:36–39)

But in those days, after that tribulation, the sun will be darkened, and the moon will not give its light, and the stars will be falling from heaven, and the powers in the heavens will be shaken. And then they will see the **Son of man coming** in clouds with great power and glory. And then He will send out the angels, and gather His elect from the four winds, from the ends of the earth to the ends of heaven. (Mark 13:24–27)

And then they will see the **Son of man coming** in a cloud with power and great glory. (Luke 21:27)

But in fact Christ has been raised from the dead, the first fruits of those who have fallen asleep. For as by a man came death, by a man has come also the resurrection of the dead. For as in Adam all die, so also in Christ shall all be made alive. But each in His own order: Christ the first fruits, then at His coming those who belong to Christ. Then comes the end, when He delivers the kingdom to God the Father after destroying every rule and every authority and power. The last enemy to be destroyed is death. (1 Cor. 15:20–26)

So is it with the resurrection of the dead. What is sown is perishable, what is raised is imperishable. It is sown in dishonor, it is raised in glory. It is sown in weakness, it is raised in power. It is sown a physical body, it is raised a spiritual body. If there is a physical body, there is also a spiritual body. As was the man of dust, so are those who are of the dust; and as is the man of heaven, so are those who are of heaven. Just as we have borne the image of the man of dust, we shall also bear the image of the man of heaven. (1 Cor. 15:42–50)

But our commonwealth is in heaven, and from it we await a Savior, the Lord Jesus Christ, who will change our lowly body to be like His glorious body. (Phil. 3:20–21)

When Christ who is our life appears, then you also will appear with Him in glory. (Col. 3:4)

For this we declare to you by the word of the Lord, that we who are alive, who are left until the coming of the Lord, shall not precede those who have fallen asleep. For the **Lord Himself will descend** from heaven with a cry of command, with the archangel's call, and with the sound of the trumpet of God. And the dead in Christ will rise first, then we who are alive, who are left, shall be caught up together with them in the clouds to meet the Lord in the air; and so we shall always be with the Lord. (1 Thess. 4:15–17)

But as to the times and the seasons, brethren, you have no need to have anything written to you. For you yourselves know well that the day of the Lord will come like a thief in the night. (1 Thess. 5:1–2)

And to grant rest with us to you who are afflicted, when the Lord Jesus is revealed from heaven with His mighty angels in flaming fire, inflicting vengeance upon those who do not know God and upon those who do not obey the gospel of our Lord Jesus. They shall suffer the punishment of eternal destruction and exclusion from the presence of the Lord and from the glory of His might, when He comes on that day to be glorified in His saints, and to be marveled at in all who have believed. (2 Thess. 1:7–10)

But understand this, that in the last days there will come times of stress. (2 Tim. 3:1)

Awaiting our blessed hope, the appearing of the glory of our great God and Savior Jesus Christ. (Titus 2:13)

For Christ has entered, into heaven itself, now to appear in the presence of God on our behalf. So **Christ**, having been offered once to bear the sins of many, **will appear** a second time, not to deal with sin but to save those who are eagerly waiting for Him. (Heb. 9:24, 28)

The end of all things is at hand; therefore, keep sane and sober for your prayers. (1 Pet. 4:7)

But by the same word the heavens and earth that now exist have been stored up for fire, being kept until the day of judgment and destruction of ungodly men. But the day of the Lord will come like a thief, and then the heavens will pass away with a loud noise, and the elements will be dissolved with fire, and the earth and the works that are upon it will be burned up. (2 Pet. 3:7, 10)

Beloved, we are God's children now; it does not yet appear what we shall be, but we know that when He appears we shall be like Him, for we shall see Him as He is. (1 John 3:2)

Behold, **He is coming with the clouds**, and every eye will see Him, every one who pierced Him; and all tribes of the earth will wail on account of Him. (Rev. 1:7)

Confirmation/Clarity

I am the Lord, who **confirms** the word of His servant. (Isa. 44:26)

Truly, truly I say to you, if you ask anything of the Father, He will give it to you in My name. (John 16:23)

That every word may be **confirmed** by the evidence of two or three witnesses. (Matt. 18:16)

And they went forth and preached everywhere, while the Lord worked with them and **confirmed** the message by the signs that attended it. (Mark 16:20)

Any charge must be sustained by the evidence of two or three witnesses. (2 Cor. 13:1)

Confusion

To Thee they cried, and were saved; in Thee they trusted, and were not **disappointed**. (Ps. 22:5)

In Thee, O Lord, do I take refuge; let me never be put to **shame**! (Ps. 71:1)

A man without **self-control** is like a city broken into and left without walls. (Prov. 25:28)

For the Lord God help me; therefore, I have not been **confounded**. (Isa. 50:7)

For God is not a God of **confusion** but of peace. (1 Cor. 14:33)

For where jealousy and selfish ambition exist, there will be **disorder** and every vile practice. (James 3:16)

Covenant

But I will establish My **covenant** with you. (Gen. 6:18)

Then God said to Noah and to his sons with him "Behold, I establish My **covenant** with you and your descendants after you—I establish My covenant with you,—I set my bow in the cloud, and it shall be a sign of the **covenant** between Me and the earth. (Gen. 9:8, 11, 13)

I also established My **covenant** with them, Moreover I have heard the groaning of the people of Israel whom the Egyptians hold in bondage and I have remembered My **covenant**. (Exod. 6:4–5)

Now therefore, if you will obey My voice and keep My **covenant**, you shall be My own possession among all peoples. (Exod. 19:5)

And Moses took the blood and threw it upon the people, and said, "Behold the blood of the **covenant** which the Lord has made with you in accordance with all these words." (Exod. 24:8)

Therefore the people of Israel shall keep the Sabbath, observing the Sabbath throughout their generations, as a perpetual **covenant**. (Exod. 31:16)

Therefore say, Behold, I give to him my **covenant** of peace; and it shall be to him and to his descendants after him, the **covenant** of a perpetual priesthood. (Num. 25:12)

And He declared to you His **covenant**, which He commanded you to perform, that is, the ten commandments; and He wrote them upon two tables of stone. (Deut. 4:13)

Know therefore that the Lord your God is God, the faithful God who keeps **covenant** and steadfast love with those who love Him and keep His commandments, to a thousand generations. (Deut. 7:9)

Yea, does not my house stand so with God? For He has made with me an everlasting **covenant**, ordered in all things and secure. (2 Sam. 23:5)

O Lord, God of Israel, there is no God like Thee, in heaven above or on earth beneath, keeping **covenant** and showing steadfast love to Thy servants who walk before Thee with all their heart. (1 Kings 8:23)

And you shall not forget the **covenant** that I have made with you. (2 Kings 17:38)

I will not violate My **covenant**, or alter the word that went forth from My lips. (Ps. 89:34)

Death/Dying

But of the tree of the knowledge of good and evil you shall not eat, for in the day that you eat of it you shall **die**. (Gen. 2:17)

Whoever strikes a man so that he dies shall be put to **death**. But if a man willfully attacks another to kill him treacherously, you shall take him from My altar, that he may **die**. Whoever strikes his father or his mother shall be put to **death**. Whoever steals a man, whether he sells him or is found in possession of him, shall be put to **death**. Whoever curses his father or his mother shall be put to **death**. (Exod. 21:12, 14–17)

He who blasphemes the name of the Lord shall be put to **death**. He who kills a man shall be put to **death**. (Lev. 24:16–17)

The fathers shall not be put to **death** for the children, nor shall the children be put to **death** for the fathers; every man shall be put to **death** for his own sin. (Deut. 24:16)

See, I have set before you this day life and good, **death** and evil. (Deut. 30:15)

Even though I walk through the valley of the shadow of **death**, I fear no evil. (Ps. 23:4)

Precious in the sight of the Lord is the **death** of His saints. (Ps. 116:15)

The soul that sins shall **die**. (Ezek. 18:20)

For as the Father raises the **dead** and gives them life, so also the Son gives life to whom He will. (John 5:21)

For the wages of sin is **death**. (Rom. 6:23)

For this perishable nature must put on the imperishable, and this mortal nature must put on immortality. When the perishable puts on the imperishable, and the mortal puts on immortality, then shall come to pass the saying that is written: "**Death** is swallowed up in victory." O **death,** where is thy victory? O **death,** where is thy sting? The sting of **death** is sin. (1 Cor. 15:53–56)

For to me to live is Christ, and to **die** is gain. (Phil. 1:21)

And just as it is appointed for men to **die** once, and after that comes judgment. (Heb. 9:27)

Defilement/Rebellion

So Jacob said to his household and to all who were with him, Put away the foreign gods that are among you, and purify yourselves, and change your garments. (Gen. 35:2)

Whoever lies with a beast shall be put to death. (Exod. 22:19)

And you shall take no bribe, for a bribe blinds the officials. (Exod. 23:8)

You shall not approach a woman to uncover her nakedness while she is in her menstrual uncleanness. And you shall not lie carnally with your neighbor's wife, and defile yourself with her. You shall not give any of your children to devote them by fire to Molech. You shall not lie with a male as with a woman, it is an abomination. You shall not lie with any beast and defile yourself with it, neither shall any woman give herself to a beast to lie with it; it is perversion. (Lev. 18:19–23)

For every one who curses his father or his mother shall be put to death; he has cursed his father or his mother, his blood is upon him. (Lev. 20:9)

If a man lies with a male as with a woman, both of them have committed an abomination; they shall be put to death, their blood is upon them. If a man takes a wife and her mother also, it is wickedness; they shall be burned with fire, If a man lies with a beast, he shall be put to death. If a woman approaches any beast and lies with it, you shall kill the woman and the beast; their blood is upon them. If a man takes his sister, and sees her nakedness, it is a shameful thing, and they shall be cut off in the sight of the children of their people. (Lev. 20:13–17)

You shall not **defile** the land in which you live. (Lev. 35:34)

Thus they became **unclean** by their acts, and played the harlot in their doings. (Ps. 106:39)

And he said, "What comes out of a man is what **defiles** a man." (Mark 7:20)

But understand this, that in the last days there will come times of stress. For men will be lovers of self, lovers of money, proud, arrogant, abusive, disobedient to their parents, ungrateful, unholy, inhuman, implacable, slanderers, profligates, fierce, haters of good, treacherous, reckless, swollen with conceit, lovers of pleasure rather than lovers of God, holding the form of religion but denying the power of it. (2 Tim. 3:1–5)

To the pure all things are pure, but to the **corrupt** and unbelieving nothing is pure; their very minds and consciences are corrupted. (Titus 1:15)

I was provoked with that generation, and said, "they always go astray in their hearts; they have not known My ways. As I swore in My wrath, they shall never enter My rest." Take care, brethren, lest there be in any of you an evil, unbelieving heart, leading you to fall away from the living God. while it is said, "Today, when you hear His voice, do not harden your hearts as in the **rebellion**." (Heb. 3:10–12, 15)

See to it that no one fail to obtain the grace of God; that no "root of bitterness" spring up and cause trouble, and by it the many become **defiled;** that no one be immoral or irreligious. (Heb. 12:15)

Therefore put away all **filthiness** and rank growth of **wickedness** and receive with meekness the implanted word, which is able to save your souls. (James 1:21)

The tongue is an unrighteous world among our members, staining the whole body, setting on fire the cycle of nature, and set on fire by hell. But no human being can tame the tongue—a restless **evil,** full of deadly poison. With it we bless the Lord and Father, and with it we curse men. From the same mouth come blessing and cursing. (James 3:6, 8–10)

For where jealousy and selfish ambition exist, there will be disorder and every **vile** practice. (James 3:16)

Then the Lord knows how to rescue the godly from trial, and to keep the unrighteous under punishment until the day of judgment, and especially those who indulge in the lust of **defiling** passion and despise authority. (2 Pet. 2:9–10)

For if, after they have escaped the **defilements** of the world through the knowledge of our Lord and Savior Jesus Christ, they are again entangled in them and overpowered, the last state has become worse for them than the first. (2 Pet. 2:20)

Do not love the world or the things in the world. If any one loves the world, love for the Father is not in him. For all that is in the world, the **lust** of the flesh and the **lust** of the eyes and the **pride** of life, is not of the Father but is of the world. (1 John 2:15–16)

He who does not love abides in death. (1 John 3:14)

Little children, keep yourselves from idols. (1 John 5:21)

Devil

Then the God of peace will soon crush **Satan** under your feet. (Rom. 16:20)

What I have forgiven, if I have forgiven anything, has been for your sake in the presence of Christ, to keep **Satan** from gaining the advantage over us; for we are not ignorant of his designs. (2 Cor. 2:10–11)

And give no opportunity to the **devil**. (Eph. 4:27)

And then the **lawless one** will be revealed, and the Lord Jesus will slay him with the breath of His mouth and destroy him by His appearing and His coming. (2 Thess. 2:8)

Now the Spirit expressly says that in later times some will depart from the faith by giving heed to **deceitful spirits** and doctrines of **demons**. (1 Tim. 4:1)

Since therefore the children share in flesh and blood, He Himself likewise partook of the same nature, that through death He might destroy him who has the power of death, that is, the **devil**. (Heb. 2:14)

Submit yourselves therefore to God. Resist the **devil** and he will flee from you. (James 4:7)

Who is the liar but he who denies that Jesus is the Christ? This is the **antichrist,** he who denies the Father and the Son. (1 John 2:22)

Little children, let no one deceive you. He who commits sin is of the **devil;** for the **devil** has sinned from the beginning. (1 John 3:7–8)

And the great **dragon** was thrown down, that ancient **serpent**, who is called the **Devil** and **Satan**, the deceiver of the whole world. But woe to you, O earth and sea, for the **devil** has come down to you in great wrath, because he knows that his time is short! (Rev. 12:9, 12)

And he seized the **dragon**, that ancient **serpent,** who is the **Devil** and **Satan**, and bound him for a thousand years, and threw him into the pit, and shut it and sealed it over him, that he should deceive the nations no more. (Rev. 20:2)

Discernment

Give Thy servant therefore an understanding mind to govern Thy people, that I may **discern** between good and evil. (1 Kings 3:9)

Thou knowest when I sit down and when I rise up; Thou **discernest** my thoughts from afar. (Ps. 139:2)

The unspiritual man does not receive the gifts of the Spirit of God, for they are folly to him, and he is not able to understand them because they are spiritually **discerned**. (1 Cor. 2:14)

Beloved, do not believe every spirit, but **test the spirits** to see whether they are of God; for many false prophets have gone out into the world. (1 John 4:1)

Discouragement

Be strong and of good courage, do not fear or be in dread of them, for it is the Lord your God who goes with you; He will not fail you or forsake you. It is the Lord who goes before you; He will be with you, He will not fail you or forsake you do not fear or be **dismayed**. (Deut. 31:6, 8)

Then they cried to the Lord in their trouble, and He delivered them from their **distress**. (Ps. 107:19)

Fear not, for I am with you, be not **dismayed**, for I am your God. (Isa. 41:10)

For I, the Lord your God, hold your right hand; it is I who say to you, "Fear not, I will help you." (Isa. 41:13)

Come to Me, all who labor and are heavy laden, and I will give you rest. (Matt. 11:28)

Have no **anxiety** about anything, but in everything by prayer and supplication with thanksgiving let your requests be made known to God. (Phil. 4:6)

Brethren, do not be **weary** in well-doing. (2 Thess. 3:13)

Therefore do not throw away your confidence, which has a great reward. (Heb. 10:35)

The Lord is my helper, I will not be **afraid**. (Heb. 13:6)

Divorce

When a man takes a wife and marries her, if then she finds no favor in his eyes because has found some indecency in her, and he writes her a bill of **divorce** and puts it in her hand and sends her out of his house, and she departs out of his house, and if she goes and becomes another man's wife, and the latter husband dislikes her and writes her a bill of **divorce** and puts it in her hand and sends her out of his house or if the latter husband dies, who took her to be his wife, then her former husband may not take her again to be his wife, after she has been defiled; for that is an abomination before the Lord. (Deut. 1–4)

Remember not the former things, nor consider the things of old. Behold, I am doing a new thing; now it springs forth, do you not perceive it? (Isa. 43:18–19)

For I hate **divorce,** say the Lord the God of Israel. (Mal. 2:16)

Whoever **divorces** his wife, let him give her a certificate of **divorce**. But I say to you that every one who **divorces** his wife, except on the ground of unchastity, makes her an adulteress. (Matt. 5:31, 32)

He said to them, for your hardness of heart Moses allowed you to **divorce** your wives, but from the beginning it was not so. And I say to you: whoever **divorces** his wife, except for unchastity, and marries another commits adultery. (Matt. 19:8–9)

And He said to them, "Whoever **divorces** his wife and marries another, commits adultery against her; and if she **divorces** her husband and marries another, she commits adultery. (Mark 10:11–12)

Every one who **divorces** his wife and marries another commits adultery, and he who marries a woman **divorced** from her husband commits adultery. (Luke 16:18)

Thus a married woman is bound by law to her husband as long as he lives; but if her husband dies she is discharged from the law concerning the husband. Accordingly, she will be called an adulteress if she lives with another man while her husband is alive. But if her husband dies she is free from that law, and if she marries another man she is not an adulteress. (Rom. 7:2–3)

To the married I give charge, not I but the Lord, that the wife should not separate from her husband and that the husband should not **divorce** his wife. To the rest I say, not the Lord, that if any brother has a wife who is an unbeliever, and she consents to live with him, he should not **divorce** her. If any woman has a husband who is an unbeliever, and he consents to live with her, she should not **divorce** him. For the unbelieving husband is consecrated through his wife, and the unbelieving wife is consecrated through her husband. But if the unbelieving partner desires to separate, let it be so; in such a case the brother or sister is not bound. For God has called us to peace. (1 Cor. 7:10–15)

A wife is bound to her husband as long as he lives. If the husband dies, she is free to be married to whom she wishes, only in the Lord. (1 Cor. 7:39)

Therefore, if anyone is in Christ, he is a new creation; the old has passed away, behold, the new has come. (2 Cor. 5:17)

Doubt

Be still, and know that I am God. (Ps. 46:10)

Jesus immediately reached out His hand and caught him, saying to him, "O man of little faith, why did you **doubt**?" (Matt. 14:31)

And Jesus said to him, "If you can! All things are possible to him who believes." Immediately the father of the child cried out and said, "I believe; help my **unbelief**!" (Mark 9:23–24)

Take care, brethren, lest there be in any of you an evil, **unbelieving** heart, leading you to fall away from the living God. (Heb. 3:12)

But let him ask in faith, with no **doubting**, for he who doubts is like a wave of the sea that is driven and tossed by the wind. For that person must not suppose that a double minded man, unstable in all his ways, will receive anything from the Lord. (James 1:6–8)

And convince some, who **doubt**; save some, by snatching them out of the fire. (Jude 22–23)

Eating/Drinking

Every moving thing that lives shall be food for you; and as I gave you the green plants, I give you everything. Only you shall not **eat** flesh with its life, that is, its blood. (Gen. 9:3–4)

You shall not delay to offer from the fullness of your harvest and from the outflow of your presses. (Exod. 22:29)

You shall serve the Lord your God, and I will bless your bread and your water. (Exod. 23:25)

Say to the people of Israel, you shall **eat** no fat, of ox, or sheep, or goat. (Lev. 7:23)

If any man of the house of Israel or of the strangers that sojourn among them **eats** any blood, I will set my face against that person who **eats** blood, For the life of the flesh is in the blood. (Lev. 17:10–11)

You shall not **eat** any flesh with the blood in it. (Lev. 19:26)

And the Lord said to Moses, "Say to the people of Israel, when either a man or a woman makes a special vow, the vow of a Nazarite, to separate himself to the Lord, he shall separate himself from wine and strong **drink;** he shall **drink** no vinegar made from wine or strong **drink**, and shall not **drink** any juice of grapes or **eat** grapes, fresh or dried. All the days of his separation he shall **eat** nothing that is produced by the grapevine, not even the seeds or the skins." (Num. 6:1–4)

And you shall **eat** and be full, and you shall bless the Lord your God for the good land He has given you. (Deut. 8:10)

You shall not **eat** any abominable thing. (Deut. 14:3)

Of all that are in the waters you may **eat** these: whatever has fins and scales you may **eat**. (Deut. 14:9)

You shall not **eat** anything that dies of itself. (Deut. 14:21)

Do not **eat** the bread of a man who is stingy; do not desire his delicacies. For he is like one who is inwardly reckoning. **Eat** and **drink**! He says to you; but his heart is not with you. (Prov. 23:6–7)

Whoever **eats** the bread or **drinks** the cup of the Lord in an unworthy manner will be guilty of profaning the body and blood of the Lord. Let a man examine himself, and so **eat** of the bread and **drink** of the cup. For any one who **eats** and **drinks** without discerning the body **eats** and **drinks** judgment upon himself. (1 Cor. 11:27–29, The Lord's Supper)

So then, my brethren, when you come together to **eat**, wait for one another—if any one is hungry, let him **eat** at home—lest you come together to be condemned. (1 Cor. 11:33, 34)

Therefore let no one pass judgment on you in questions of food and **drink** or with regard to a festival or a new moon or a Sabbath. (Col. 2:16)

No longer **drink** only water, but use a little wine for the sake of your stomach and your frequent ailments. (1 Tim. 5:23)

Endurance

Not that I complain of want; for I have learned in whatever state I am, to be content. (Phil. 4:11)

I can do all things in Him who strengthens me. (Phil. 4:13)

For to this end we toil and strive, because we have our hope set on the living God. (1 Tim. 4:10)

Do not be ashamed then of testifying to our Lord, nor of me His prisoner, but share in suffering for the gospel in the power of God. (2 Tim. 1:8)

If we **endure,** we shall also reign with Him; if we deny Him, He also will deny us. (2 Tim. 2:12)

As for you, always be steady, **endure** suffering, do the work of an evangelist, fulfil your ministry. (2 Tim. 4:5)

And thus Abraham, having patiently **endured**, obtained the promise. (Heb. 6:15)

But recall the former days when, after you were enlightened, you **endured** a hard struggle with sufferings, For you have need of **endurance**, so that you may do the will of God and receive what is promised. (Heb. 10:32, 36)

Therefore, since we are surrounded by so great a cloud of witnesses, let us also lay aside every weight, and sin which clings so closely, and let us run with perseverance the race that is set before us, looking to Jesus the pioneer and perfecter of our faith, who for the joy that was set before Him **endured** the cross, despising the shame, and is seated at the right hand of the throne of God. It is for discipline that you have to **endure**. (Heb. 12:1–3, 7)

Count it all joy, my brethren, when you meet various trials, for you know that the testing of your faith produces **steadfastness,** and let steadfastness have its full effect, that you may be perfect and complete, lacking in nothing. (James 1:2–4)

Blessed is the man who **endures** trial, for when he has stood the test he will receive the crown of life which God has promised to those who love Him. (James 1:12)

I know your works, your love and faith and service and patient **endurance**. (Rev. 2:19)

Because you have kept My word of patient **endurance**, I will keep you from the hour of trial which is coming on the whole world, He who conquers, I will make him a pillar in the temple of My God. (Rev. 3:10, 12)

Here is a call for the **endurance** of the saints, those who keep the commandments of God and the faith of Jesus. (Rev. 14:12)

Evil

The Lord saw that the wickedness of man was great in the earth, and that every imagination of the thoughts of his heart was only **evil** continually. (Gen. 6:5)

The Lord said in His heart, "I will never again curse the ground because of man, for the imagination of man's heart is **evil** from his youth." (Gen. 8:21)

As for you, you meant **evil** against me; but God meant it for good, to bring it about that many people should be kept alive, as they are today. (Gen. 50:20)

You shall not follow a multitude to do **evil**. (Exod. 23:2)

Let not the anger of my lord burn hot; you know the people, that they are set on **evil**. (Exod. 32:22)

And the Lord's anger was kindled against Israel, and He made them wander in the wilderness forty years, until all the generation that had done **evil** in the sight of the Lord was consumed. (Num. 32:13)

So you shall purge the **evil** from the midst of you. (Deut. 19:19)

See, I have set before you this day life and good, death and **evil**. (Deut. 30:15)

And I will surely hide my face in that day on account of all the **evil** which they have done, because they have turned to other gods. (Deut. 31:18)

And in the days to come **evil** will befall you, because you will do what is **evil** in the sight of the Lord, provoking Him to anger through the work of your hands. (Deut. 31:29)

And the people of Israel did what was **evil** in the sight of the Lord, forgetting the Lord their God, and serving the Baals and the Asheroth. (Judg. 3:7)

Turn from your **evil** ways and keep My commandments and My statutes in accordance with all the law which I commanded your fathers. (2 Kings 17:13)

For thou art not a God who delights in wickedness; **evil** may not sojourn with thee. (Ps. 5:4)

Let no **evil** talk come out of your mouths, but only such as is good for edifying as fits the occasion. (Eph. 4:29)

For God cannot be tempted with **evil** and He Himself tempts no one. (James 1:13)

Do not return **evil** for **evil** or reviling for reviling; but on the contrary bless, let him turn away from **evil** and do right; But the face of the Lord is against those that do **evil**. (1 Pet. 3:9, 11, 12)

Beloved, do not imitate **evil** but imitate good. He who does good is of God; he who does **evil** has not seen God. (3 John 11)

Let the evildoer still do **evil**. (Rev. 22:11)

Faith

He will guard the feet of His **faithful** ones. (1 Sam. 2:9)

The Lord rewards every man for his righteousness and his **faithfulness**. (1 Sam. 26:23)

But He knows the way that I take; when He has tried me, I shall come forth as gold. (Job 23:10)

According to our **faith** be it done to you. (Matt. 9:29)

O woman, great is your **faith!** Be it done for you as you desire. (Matt. 15:28)

And whatever you ask in prayer, you will receive, if you have **faith**. (Matt. 21:22)

For God so loved the world that He gave His only Son, that whoever **believes** in Him should not perish but have eternal life. (John 3:16)

Jesus said to them, "I am the bread of life; he who comes to Me shall not hunger, and he who believes in Me shall never thirst. For this is the will of My Father, that every one who sees the Son and **believes** in Him should have eternal life." (John 6:35, 40)

Jesus said to her, "Did I not tell you that if you would **believe** you would see the glory of God?" (John 11:40)

Truly, truly, I say to you, he who **believes** in Me will also do the works that I do. (John 14:12)

And to one who does not work but trusts him who justifies the ungodly, his **faith** is reckoned as righteousness. (Rom. 4:5)

As it is written, "I have made you the father of many nations"—in the presence of the God in whom he **believed**, who gives life to the dead and calls into existence the things that do not exist. (Rom. 4:17)

The word is near you, on your lips and in your heart (that is the word of **faith** which we preach); because if you confess with your lips that Jesus is Lord and believe in your heart that

God raised him from the dead, you will be saved. (Rom. 10:8)

So **faith** comes from what is heard, and what is heard comes by the preaching of Christ. (Rom. 10:17)

To think with sober judgment, each according to the measure of **faith** which God has assigned him. (Rom. 12:3)

That your **faith** might not rest in the wisdom of men but in the power of God. (1 Cor. 2:5)

And be found in him, not having a righteousness of my own, based on law, but that which is through **faith** in Christ, the righteousness from God that depends on **faith**. (Phil. 3:8–11)

Now Moses was **faithful** in all God's house as a servant to testify to the things that were to be spoken later, but Christ was **faithful** over God's house as a son. (Heb. 3:5)

But my righteous one shall live by **faith,** and if he shrinks back, my soul has no pleasure in him. But we are not of those who shrink back and are destroyed, but of those who have **faith** and keep their souls. (Heb. 10:38, 39)

Now **faith** is the assurance of things hoped for, the conviction of things not seen. By **faith**, we understand that the world was created by the word of God, so that what is seen was made out of things which do not appear. (Heb. 11:1, 3)

And without **faith** it is impossible to please Him. (Heb. 11:6)

But let him ask in **faith,** with no doubting, for he who doubts is like a wave of the sea that is driven and tossed by the wind. (James 1:6)

What does it profit, my brethren, if a man says he has **faith** but has not works? Can his **faith** save him? So **faith** by itself, if it has no works, is dead. (James 2:14, 17)

And the prayer of **faith** will save the sick man, and the Lord will raise him up; and if he has committed sins, he will be forgiven. (James 5:15)

Beloved, if our hearts do not condemn us, we have **confidence** before God; and we receive from Him whatever we ask. (1 John 3:21, 22)

Little children, you are of God, and have overcome them; for He who is in you is greater than he who is in the world. (1 John 4:4)

For whatever is born of God overcomes the world; and this is the victory that overcomes the world, our **faith**. (1 John 5:4)

Be **faithful** unto death, and I will give you the crown of life. (Rev. 2:10)

False Doctrine/Teachers

Then Pharaoh summoned the wise men and the **sorcerers;** and they also, the **magicians** of Egypt, did the same by their secret arts. (Exod. 7:11)

You shall not permit a **sorceress** to live. Whoever sacrifices to any god, save to the Lord only, shall be utterly destroyed. (Exod. 22:18, 20)

Take heed to all that I have said to you; and make no mention of the names of other gods, nor let such be heard out of your mouth. for if you serve their god, it will surely be a snare to you. (Exod. 23:13, 33)

Do not turn to **mediums** or **wizards**; do not seek them out, to be defiled by them. (Lev. 19:31)

If a person turns to **mediums** and **wizards,** playing the harlot after them, I will set my face against that person, and will cut him off from among his people. A man or a woman who is a **medium** or a **wizard** shall be put to death. (Lev. 20:6, 27)

So Israel yoked himself to **Baal of Peor**. And the anger of the Lord was kindled against Israel; And Moses said to the judges of Israel, Every one of you slay his men who have yoked themselves to **Baal of Peor**. (Num. 25:3, 5)

If a **prophet** arises among you, or a **dreamer of dreams**, and gives you a sign or a wonder, and the sign or wonder which he tells you comes to pass, and if he says, "Let us go after other gods," which you have not known, and "let us serve them," you shall not listen to the words of that prophet or to that dreamer of dreams; for the Lord your God is testing you, to know whether you love the Lord your God with all your heart and with all your soul. But that **prophet** or that **dreamer of dreams** shall be put to death, because he has taught rebellion against the Lord your God. (Deut. 13:1–3, 5)

If your brother, or your son, or daughter, or wife, or friend entices you secretly, saying "Let us go and serve other gods," which neither you nor your fathers have known, some of the gods of the peoples that are round about you, whether near you or far off from you, you shall not yield to him or listen to him, nor shall your eye pity him, nor shall you spare him, nor shall you conceal him; but you shall kill him; because he sought to draw you away from the Lord your God. (Deut. 13:6–10)

But the prophet who presumes to speak a word in My name which I have not commanded him to speak, or who speaks in the name of **other gods**, that same prophet shall die. (Deut. 18:20)

If you forsake the Lord and serve **foreign gods**, then He will turn and do you harm, and consume you, after having done you good. (Josh. 24:20)

And the people of Israel did what was evil in the sight of the Lord and served the **Baals;** They forsook the Lord, and served the **Baals** and the **Ashtaroth**. (Judg. 2:11, 13)

Beware of **false prophets**, who come to you in sheep's clothing but inwardly are ravenous wolves. You will know them by their fruits. (Matt. 7:15)

So that we may no longer be children, tossed to and fro and carried about with every wind of doctrine, by the cunning of men, by their craftiness in deceitful wiles. (Eph. 4:14)

But test everything; hold fast what is good, abstain from every form of evil. (1 Thess. 5:21–22)

The coming of the lawless one by the activity of **Satan** will be with all power and with pretended signs and wonders, and with all wicked deception for those who are to perish, because they refused to love the truth and so be saved. (2 Thess. 2:9)

Certain persons by swerving from these have wandered away into vain discussion, desiring to be teachers of the law, without understanding either what they are saying or the things about which they make assertions. (1 Tim. 1:6)

For the time is coming when people will not endure sound teaching, but having itching ears they will accumulate for themselves teachers to suit their own likings, and will turn away from listening to the truth and wander into **myths**. (2 Tim. 4:3–4)

Do not be led away by diverse and **strange teachings**; for it is well that the heart be strengthened by grace. (Heb. 13:9)

But **false prophets** also arose among the people, just as there will be false teachers among you, who will secretly bring in **destructive heresies**, even denying the Master who brought them, bringing upon themselves swift destruction. And many will follow their licentiousness, and because of them the way of truth will be reviled. And in their greed, they will exploit you with false words. (2 Pet. 2:1–3)

They have eyes full of adultery, insatiable for sin. They entice unsteady souls. They have hearts trained in greed. Accursed children! Forsaking the right way they have gone astray; they have followed the way of **Balaam**, the son of Beor, who loved gain from wrongdoing. (2 Pet. 2:14)

Beloved, do not believe every spirit, but test the spirits to see whether they are of God; for many **false prophets** have gone out into the world. By this you know the Spirit of God: every spirit which confesses that Jesus Christ has come in the flesh is of God, and every spirit which does not confess Jesus is not of God. This is the spirit of antichrist, of which you heard that it was coming, and now it is in the world already. (1 John 4:1–3)

For many deceivers have gone out into the world, men who will not acknowledge the coming of Jesus Christ in the flesh; such a one is the **deceiver** and the **antichrist**. Any one who goes ahead and does not abide in the doctrine of Christ does not have God; If any one comes to you and does not bring this doctrine, do not receive him into the house or give him any greetings; for he who greets him shares his wicked work. (2 John 7, 9, 10–11)

Just as Sodom and Gomorrah and the surrounding cities, which likewise acted immorally and indulged in unnatural lust, serve as an example by undergoing a punishment of eternal fire. They said to you, "In the last time there will be scoffers, following their own ungodly passions." It is these who set up divisions, worldly people, devoid of the Spirit. (Jude 7, 18–19)

And now you cannot bear evil men but have tested those who call themselves apostles but are not, and found them to be false. But I have a few things against you, you have some there who hold the teaching of **Balaam**, who taught Balak to put a stumbling block before the sons of Israel, that they might eat food sacrificed to idols and practice immorality. (Rev. 2:2, 14)

But I have this against you, that you tolerate the woman **Jezebel**, who calls herself a prophetess and is teaching and beguiling my servant to practice immorality and to eat food sacrificed to idols. (Rev. 2:20)

This calls for wisdom; let him who has understanding reckon the number of the **beast**, for it is a human number, its number is six hundred and sixty-six. (666) (Rev. 13:18)

And the **beast** was captured, and with it the **false prophet** who in its presence had worked the signs by which he deceived those who had received the mark of the beast and those who worshiped its image. (Rev. 19:20)

But as for the cowardly, the faithless, the polluted, as for murderers, fornicators, **sorcerers, idolaters,** and all liars, their lot shall be in the lake that burns with fire and sulphur, which is the second death. (Rev. 21:8)

Outside are the dogs and **sorcerers** and fornicators and murderers and **idolaters,** and every one who loves and practices falsehood. (Rev. 22:15)

Family (Children)

The Lord our God be with us, as He was with our fathers; may He not leave us or forsake us; that He may incline our hearts to Him, to walk in all His ways, and to keep His commandments, His statutes, and His ordinances. (1 Kings 8:57–58)

Give Thy strength to Thy servant, and save the **son** of Thy handmaid. (Ps. 86:16)

The **children** of Thy servants shall dwell secure; their posterity shall be established before Thee. (Ps. 102:28)

But the steadfast love of the Lord is from everlasting to everlasting upon those who fear Him, and His righteousness to **children's children.** (Ps. 103:17)

Hear, my **son**, your father's instruction and reject not your mother's teaching; for they are a fair garland for your head, and pendants for your neck. (Prov. 1:8)

My **son,** do not despise the Lord's discipline or be weary of His reproof, for the Lord reproves Him whom He loves, as a father the **son** in whom He delights. (Prov. 3:11–12)

My **son**, be attentive to My words; incline your ear to My sayings. (Prov. 4:20)

He who spares the rod hates his **son,** but he who loves him is diligent to discipline him. (Prov. 13:24)

Discipline your **son** while there is hope; do not set your heart on his destruction. (Prov. 19:18)

A good name is to be chosen rather than great riches. (Prov. 22:1)

Train up a **child** in the way he should go, and when he is old he will not depart from it. (Prov. 22:6)

Folly is bound up in the heart of a **child,** but the rod of discipline drives it far from him. (Prov. 22:15)

Do not withhold discipline from a **child**; if you beat him with a rod, he will not die. If you beat him with the rod you will save his life from Sheol. (Prov. 23:13–14)

The rod and reproof give wisdom, but a **child** left to himself brings shame to his mother. (Prov. 29:15)

Discipline your **son,** and he will give you rest; he will give delight to your heart. (Prov. 29:17)

I will pour my Spirit upon your **descendants**, and my blessing on your **offspring**. (Isa. 44:3)

Before I formed you in the womb I knew you, and before you were born I consecrated you. (Jer. 1:4)

I am the Lord your God, who teaches you to profit, who leads you in the way you should go. (Isa. 48:17)

For I will contend with those who contend with you, and I will save your **children**. (Isa. 49:25)

All your **sons** shall be taught by the Lord, and great shall be the prosperity of your **sons**. (Isa. 54:13)

And as for me, this is my covenant with them, says the Lord: my spirit which is upon you, and my words which I have put in your mouth, shall not depart out of your mouth, or out of the mouth of your **children**, or out of the mouth of your **children's children,** says the Lord, from this time forth and for evermore. (Isa. 59:21)

Let the **children** come to me, and do not hinder them; for to such belongs the kingdom of God. (Luke 18:16)

Fathers, do not provoke your **children**, lest they become discouraged. (Col. 3:21)

Favor

And the Lord had given the people **favor** in the sight of the Egyptians, so that they let them have what they asked. (Exod. 12:36)

This very thing that you have spoken I will do; for you have found **favor** in my sight, and I know you by name. I will make all my goodness pass before you, and will proclaim before you my name "The Lord" and I will be gracious to whom I will be gracious, and will show mercy on whom I will show mercy. (Exod. 33:17, 19)

And the Lord said, "Behold, there is a place by Me where you shall stand upon the rock; and while My glory passes by I will put you in a cleft of the rock, and I will cover you with My hand until I have passed by." (Exod. 33:21)

And he said, If now I have found **favor** in Thy sight, O Lord, let the Lord, I pray Thee, go in the midst of us, and pardon our iniquity and our sin, and take us for Thy inheritance. (Exod. 34:9)

Arise, O Lord, and let Thy enemies be scattered; and let them that hate Thee flee before Thee. (Num. 10:35)

If thou wilt deal thus with me, kill me at once, if I find **favor** in Thy sight, that I may not see my wretchedness. (Num. 11:15)

And she said, "Let your maidservant find **favor** in your eyes." (1 Sam. 1:18)

Jabez called on the God of Israel, saying, "Oh that Thou wouldst bless me and enlarge my border, and that Thy hand might be with me, and that Thou wouldst keep me from harm so that it might not hurt me!" And God granted what he asked. (1 Chron. 4:10)

You will make your prayer to Him, and He will hear you; and you will pay your vows. You will decide on a matter, and it will be established for you, and light will shine on your ways. (Job 22:27–28)

For Thou dost bless the righteous, O Lord; Thou dost cover him with **favor** as with a shield. (Ps. 5:12)

Truly, truly I say to you, if you ask anything of the Father, He will give it to you in My name. (John 16:23)

Fear

Do not **fear** or be dismayed. (Deut. 1:21)

It is the Lord who goes before you; He will be with you, He will not fail you or forsake you; do not **fear** or be dismayed. (Deut. 31:8)

But you shall **fear** the Lord, who brought you out of the land of Egypt with great power and with an outstretched arm; but you shall **fear** the Lord your God, and He will deliver you out of the hand of all your enemies. (2 Kings 17:36, 39)

Even though I walk through the valley of the shadow of death, I **fear** no evil; for Thou art with me; Thy rod and Thy staff, they comfort me. (Ps. 23:4)

The Lord is my light and my salvation; whom shall I **fear**? The Lord is the stronghold of my life; of whom shall I be afraid? (Ps. 27:1)

I sought the Lord, and He answered me, and delivered me from all my **fears**. (Ps. 34:4)

You will not **fear** the terror of the night, nor the arrow that flies by day. (Ps. 91:5)

The **fear** of man lays a snare, but he who trusts in the Lord is safe. (Prov. 29:25)

Fear not, for I am with you, be not dismayed, for I am your God. (Isa. 41:10)

Why even the hairs of your head are all numbered. **Fear** not; you are of more value than many sparrows. (Luke 12:7)

For you did not receive the spirit of slavery to fall back into **fear**, but you have received the spirit of sonship. (Rom. 8:15)

For God did not give us a spirit of **timidity** but a spirit of power and love and self-control. (2 Tim. 1:7)

There is no **fear** in love, but perfect love casts out **fear**. For **fear** has to do with punishment, and he who **fears** is not perfected in love. (1 John 4:18)

Festivals/Observances—Sabbath

The blood shall be a sign for you, upon the houses where you are; and when I see the blood, I will pass over you, and no plague shall fall upon you to destroy you, when I smite the land of Egypt. This day shall be for you a **memorial day**, and you shall keep it as a feast to the Lord; throughout your generations you shall observe it as an ordinance for ever. (Exod. 12:13–14)

Remember the **Sabbath** day, to keep it holy. (Exod. 20:8)

Six days you shall do your work, but on the seventh day you shall rest. (Exod. 23:12)

Three times in the year you shall keep a feast to Me. You shall keep the **feast of unleavened bread**; You shall keep the **feast of harvest**, of the first fruits of your labor, of what you sow in the field. You shall keep the **feast of ingathering** at the end of the year, when you gather in from the field the fruit of your labor. (Exod. 23:14–16)

In the first month, on the fourteenth day of the month in the evening, is the **Lord's Passover**.

And on the fifteenth day of the same month is the **feast of unleavened bread** to the Lord; seven days you shall eat unleavened bread. (Lev. 23:5, 6)

Say to the people of Israel, when you come into the land which I give you and reap its harvest, you shall bring the sheaf of the first fruits of your harvest to the priest. (Lev. 23:10)

Say to the people of Israel, in the seventh month, on the first day of the month, you shall observe a day of solemn rest, a memorial proclaimed with blasts of trumpets, a holy convocation. (Lev. 23:23)

On the tenth day of this seventh month is the **day of atonement**; it shall be for you a time of holy convocation, and you shall afflict yourselves and present an offering by fire to the Lord. (Lev. 23:26)

Say to the people of Israel, on the fifteenth day of this seventh month and for seven days is the **feast of booths** to the Lord. (Lev. 23:33)

Therefore let no one pass judgment on you in questions of food and drink or with regard to a **festival** or a new moon or a Sabbath. (Col. 2:16)

Forgiveness

Then the Lord said, "I have **pardoned**, according to your word." (Num. 14:20)

And hearken Thou to the supplication of Thy servant and of Thy people Israel, when they pray toward this place; yea, hear Thou in heaven Thy dwelling place; and when Thou hearest, **forgive**. (1 Kings 8:30)

And **forgive** Thy people who have sinned against Thee, and all their transgressions which they have committed against Thee. (1 Kings 8:50)

Let the wicked forsake his way, and the unrighteous man his thoughts; let him return to the Lord, that He may have mercy on him, and to our God, for He will abundantly **pardon**. (Isa. 55:7)

Clear Thou me from hidden faults. Keep back Thy servant also from presumptuous sins; let them not have dominion over me! (Ps. 19:12–13)

For if you **forgive** men their trespasses, your heavenly Father also will **forgive** you; but if you do not **forgive** men their trespasses, neither will your Father **forgive** your trespasses. (Matt. 6:14–15)

So also my heavenly Father will do to every one of you, if you do not **forgive** your brother from your heart. (Matt. 18:35)

And whenever you stand praying, **forgive**, if you have anything against any one; so that your Father also who is in heaven may **forgive** you your trespasses. (Mark 11:25)

If you **forgive** the sins of any, they are forgiven; if you retain the sins of any, they are retained. (John 20:23)

Let all bitterness and wrath and anger and clamor and slander be put away from you, with all malice, and be kind to one another, tenderhearted, **forgiving** one another, as God in Christ forgave you. (Eph. 4:31–32)

Gentleness

Blessed are the **meek**, for they shall inherit the earth. (Matt. 5:5)

Brethren, if a man is overtaken in any trespass, you who are spiritual should restore him in a spirit of **gentleness**. (Gal. 6:1)

But we were **gentle** among you, like a nurse taking care of her children. (1 Thess. 2:7)

And the Lord's servant must not be quarrelsome but kindly to every one, an apt teacher, forbearing, correcting his opponents with **gentleness**. (2 Tim. 2:24)

Remind them to be submissive to rulers and authorities, to be obedient, to be ready for any honest work, to speak evil of no one, to avoid quarreling, to be **gentle**, and to show perfect courtesy toward all men. (Titus 3:1–2)

Who is wise and understanding among you? By his good life let him show his works in the **meekness** of wisdom. But the wisdom from above is first pure, then peaceable, **gentle,** open to reason, full of mercy and good fruits, without uncertainty or insincerity. (James 3:13, 17)

Giants (Rephaim/Anakim/Nephilim)

The **Nephilim** were on the earth in those days, and also afterward, when the sons of God came in to the daughters of men, and they bore children to them. These were the mighty men that were of old, the men of renown. (Gen. 6:4)

Then the men who had gone up with him said, "We are not able to go up against the people; for they are stronger than we." So they brought to the people of Israel an evil report of the land which they had spied out, saying, "the land, through which we have gone to spy it out, is a land that devours its inhabitants; and all the people that we saw in it are men of great stature. And there we saw the **Nephilim** (the sons of Anak, who come from the **Nephilim**) and we seemed to ourselves like grasshoppers, and so we seemed to them." (Num. 13:31–33)

The **Emim** formerly lived there, a people great and many, as tall as the **Anakim**; like the **Anakim** they are also known as **Rephaim**, but the Moabites call them **Emim**. (Deut. 2:10–11)

That also is known as a land of **Rephaim**; Rephaim formerly lived there, but the Ammonites call them **Zamzummim**, a people great and many, and tall as the **Anakim**. (Deut. 2:20–21)

Hear, O Israel; you are to pass over the Jordan this day, to go in to dispossess nations greater and mightier than yourselves, cities great and fortified up to heaven, a people great and tall, the sons of the **Anakim,** whom you know, and of whom you have heard it said, "Who can stand before the sons of Anak?" (Deut. 9:1–2)

And Joshua came at that time, and wiped out the **Anakim** from the hill country; Joshua utterly destroyed them with their cities. There was none of the **Anakim** left in the land of the people of Israel. (Josh. 11:21, 22)

All the kingdom of Og in Bashan, who reigned in Ashtaroth and in Edrei, "he alone was left of the remnant of the **Rephaim**." (Josh. 13:12)

Now the name of Hebron formerly was Kiriatharba; this Arba was the greatest man among the **Anakim**. (Josh. 14:15)

And there came out from the camp of the Philistines a champion named Goliath, of Gath, whose height was six cubits and a span. (1 Sam. 17:4)

And Ishbibenob, one of the descendants of the **giants**, whose spear weighed three hundred shekels of bronze, and who was girded with a new sword, thought to kill David. Then Sibbecai the Hushathite slew Saph, who was one of the descendants of the **giants**. (2 Sam. 21:16, 18)

And there was again war at Gath, where there was a man of great stature, who had six fingers on each hand, and six toes on each foot, twenty four in number; and he also was descended from the **giants**. And when he taunted Israel, Jonathan the son of Shimei, David's brother, slew him. These four were descended from the **giants** in Gath; and they fell by the hand of David and by the hand of his servants. (2 Sam. 21:20–22)

And there was again war a Gath, where there was a man of great stature, who had six fingers on each hand, and six toes on each foot, twenty four in number and he also was descended from the **giants**. (1 Chron. 20:6)

Gifts of Spirit

Now there are varieties of gifts, but the same Spirit; and there are varieties of service, but the same Lord; and there are varieties of working, but it is the same God who inspires them all in every one. To each is given the manifestation of the Spirit for the common good. To one is given through the Spirit the utterance of wisdom, and to another the utterance of knowledge according to the same Spirit, to another faith by the same Spirit, to another gifts of healing by the one Spirit to another the working of miracles, to another prophecy, to another the ability to distinguish between spirits, to another various kinds of tongues, to another the interpretation of tongues. All these are inspired by one and the same Spirit, who apportions to each one individually as He wills. (1 Cor. 12:4–11)

But the fruit of the Spirit is love, joy, peace, patience, kindness, goodness, faithfulness, gentleness, and self-control. (Gal. 5:22)

Do not neglect the **gift** you have, which was given you by prophetic utterance when the council of elders laid their hands upon you. (1 Tim. 4:14)

Hence I remind you to rekindle the **gift** of God that is within you through the laying on of my hands. (2 Tim. 1:6)

While God also bore witness by signs and wonders and various miracles and by **gifts** of the Holy Spirit distributed according to His own will. (Heb. 2:4)

As each has received a **gift,** employ it for one another, as good stewards of God's varied grace: whoever speaks, as one who utters oracles of God; whoever renders service, as one who renders it by the strength which God supplies. (1 Pet. 4:10)

For the testimony of Jesus is the **spirit of prophecy**. (Rev. 19:10)

Giving/Tithing

And Abram **gave** him a tenth of everything. (Gen. 14:20)

And of all that thou **givest** me, I will **give** the tenth to thee. (Gen. 28:22)

All the **tithe** of the land, whether of the seed of the land or of the fruit of the trees, is the Lord's. (Lev. 27:30)

So shall you also present an **offering** to the Lord from all your tithes. (Num. 18:28)

You shall **give** to him freely, and your heart shall not be grudging when you **give** to him; because for this the Lord your God will bless you in all your work and in all that you undertake. For the poor will never cease out of the land; therefore, I command you, you shall open wide your hand to your brother, to the needy and to the poor, in the land. (Deut. 15:10–11)

And **pay** your vows to the Most High. (Ps. 50:14)

Honor the Lord with your substance and with the first fruits of all your produce. (Prov. 3:9)

One man **gives** freely, yet grows all the richer; another withholds what he should give, and only suffers want. A liberal man will be enriched, and one who waters will himself be watered. (Prov. 11:24–25)

He who **gives** to the poor will not want, but he who hides his eyes will get many a curse. (Prov. 28:27)

When you vow a vow to God, do not delay **paying** it; for He has no pleasure in fools. (Eccles. 5:4)

Will man rob God? Yet you are robbing Me. But you say, "How are we robbing Thee?" In your **tithes** and offerings. Bring the full **tithes** into the storehouse. (Mal. 3:8–11)

Give, and it will be given to you; good measure, pressed down, shaken together, running over, will be put into your lap. For the measure you **give** will be the measure you get back. (Luke 6:38)

Contribute to the need of the saints, practice hospitality. (Rom. 12:13)

And to him Abraham apportioned a tenth part of everything. Abraham the patriarch **gave** him a **tithe** of the spoils. Here **tithes** are received by mortal men. (Heb. 7:2, 4, 8)

God's True Kindred

You shall be men **consecrated** to me. (Exod. 22:31)

And he said to Korah and all his company, "In the morning the Lord will show who is His, and who is **holy**, and will cause him to come near to Him; him who He will choose He will cause to come near to Him." (Num. 16:5)

For you are a people **holy** to the Lord your God; the Lord your God has **chosen** you to be a people for His own possession, out of all the peoples that are on the face of the earth. (Deut. 7:6)

And the Lord has declared this day concerning you that you are a people for His **own possession**, as He has promised you, and that you are to keep all His commandments, that He will set you high above all nations that He has made, in praise and in fame and in honor, and that you shall be a people **holy** to the Lord your God, as He has spoken. (Deut. 26:18–19)

Yea, He loved His people; all those **consecrated** to Him were in His hand. (Deut. 33:3)

But David said to Abishai, "Do not destroy him; for who can put forth his hand against the Lord's **anointed**, and be guiltless?" (1 Sam. 26:9)

Great triumphs he gives to his king, and shows steadfast love to His **anointed**. (2 Sam. 22:51)

For Thou didst separate them from among all the peoples of the earth, to be Thy **heritage**, as Thou didst declare through Moses, Thy servant, when Thou didst bring our fathers out of Egypt. (1 Kings 8:53)

But know that the Lord has set apart the **godly** for Himself. (Ps. 4:3)

For God is with the generation of the **righteous**. (Ps. 14:5)

For to the man who **pleases** Him God gives wisdom and knowledge and joy. (Eccles. 2:26)

But the people who **know their God** shall stand firm and take action. (Dan. 11:32)

And it shall come to pass that **all who call** upon the name of the Lord shall be delivered; for in Mount Zion and in Jerusalem there shall be those who escape, as the Lord has said, and among the survivors shall be those whom the Lord calls. (Joel 2:32)

But to all who received Him, who believed in His name, He gave power to become **children of God**. (John 1:12)

If you **continue in My word**, you are truly My disciples. (John 8:31)

My sheep hear My voice, and I know them, and they follow Me; and I give them eternal life, and they shall never perish, and no one shall snatch them out of My hand. (John 10:27–28)

For all who are led by the Spirit of God are **sons of God**. (Rom. 8:14)

Who shall bring any charge against **God's elect**? (Rom. 8:33)

But he who is united to the Lord becomes **one spirit** with Him. (1 Cor. 6:17)

I will live in them and move among them, and I will be their God, and they shall be My people. Therefore come out from them, and be **separate** from them, says the Lord, and touch nothing unclean; then I will welcome you, and I will be a father to you, and you shall be My sons and daughters, says the Lord Almighty. (2 Cor. 6:16–18)

For in Christ Jesus you are all **sons of God**, through faith. (Gal. 3:26)

Put on then, as God's chosen ones, **holy** and **beloved**, compassion, kindness, lowliness, meekness, and patience. (Col. 3:12)

But God's firm foundation stands, bearing this seal: "The Lord knows those who are His." (2 Tim. 2:19)

Of His own will He brought us forth by the word of truth that we should be a kind of **first fruits** of His creatures. (James 1:18)

But you are a **chosen race**, a **royal priesthood**, a **holy nation**, God's own people, that you may declare the wonderful deeds of Him who called you out of darkness into His marvelous light. (1 Pet. 2:9)

See what love the Father has given us, that we should be called **children of God**; and so we are. Beloved, we are God's children now. (1 John 3:1–2)

By this it may be seen who are the **children of God**, and who are the children of the devil: whoever does not do right is not of God, nor he who does not love his brother. (1 John 3:10)

Every one **who believes** that Jesus is the Christ is a **child of God**. (1 John 5:1)

Those **whom I love**, I reprove and chasten. (Rev. 3:19)

For He is Lord of lords and King of kings, and **those with Him** are called and chosen and faithful. (Rev. 17:14)

And the angel said to me, "Write this: Blessed are **those who are invited** to the marriage supper of the Lamb." (Rev. 19:9)

He **who conquers** shall have this heritage, and I will be his God and he shall be My son. (Rev. 21:7)

Goodness

Surely **goodness** and mercy shall follow me all the days of my life. (Ps. 23:6)

Truly God is **good** to the upright, to those who are pure in heart. (Ps. 73:1)

But happy is he who is **kind** to the poor. (Prov. 14:21)

No one is **good** but God alone. (Mark 10:17)

Do you not know that God's **kindness** is meant to lead you to repentance? (Rom. 2:4)

And be **kind** to one another, tenderhearted, forgiving one another, as God in Christ forgave you. (Eph. 4:32)

Put on then, as God's chosen ones, holy and beloved, compassion, **kindness,** lowliness, meekness, and patience. (Col. 3:12)

By his **good** life let him show his works in the meekness of wisdom. (James 3:13)

For you have tasted the **kindness** of the Lord. (1 Pet. 2:3)

Grace

Paul and Barnabas spoke to them and urged them to continue in the **grace** of God. (Acts 13:43)

Through whom we have received **grace** and apostleship to bring about the obedience of faith. (Rom. 1:5)

Since all have sinned and fall short of the glory of God, they are justified by His **grace** as a gift, through the redemption which is in Christ Jesus. (Rom. 3:23, 24)

That is why it depends on faith, in order that the promise may rest on **grace** and be guaranteed to all his descendants. (Rom. 4:16)

Through Him we have obtained access to this **grace** in which we stand, and we rejoice in our hope of sharing the glory of God. (Rom. 5:2)

But by the **grace** of God I am what I am, and His **grace** toward me was not in vain. (1 Cor. 15:10)

My **grace** is sufficient for you, for My power is made perfect in weakness. (2 Cor. 12:9)

Let us then with confidence draw near to the throne of **grace**, that we may receive mercy and find **grace** to help in time of need. (Heb. 4:16)

See to it that no one fail to obtain the **grace** of God; that no root of bitterness spring up and cause trouble, and by it the many become defiled. (Heb. 12:15)

But He gives more **grace**; therefore it says, "God opposes the proud, but gives **grace** to the humble." (James 4:6)

But grow in the **grace** and knowledge of our Lord and Savior Jesus Christ. (2 Pet. 3:18)

Groanings/Speaking in Tongues

We know that the whole creation has been **groaning** in travail together until now; and not only the creation, but we ourselves, who have the first fruits of the Spirit, **groan inwardly** as we wait for adoption as sons. (Rom. 8:22)

And God has appointed in the church first apostles, second, prophets, third teachers, then workers of miracles, then healers, helpers, administrators, **speakers** in **various kinds of tongues**. Do all possess gifts of healing? Do all speak with Tongues? (1 Cor. 12:28, 30)

If I speak in the **tongues of men** and **of angels**, but have not love, I am a noisy gong or a clanging cymbal. (1 Cor. 13:1)

For one who **speaks in a tongue** speaks not to men but to God; for no one understands him but he utters mysteries in the Spirit. He who **speaks in a tongue** edifies himself, but he who prophesies edifies the church. Now, brethren, if I come to you **speaking in tongues**, how shall I benefit you unless I bring you some revelation or knowledge or prophecy or teaching? (1 Cor. 14:2, 4, 6)

Therefore, he who **speaks in a tongue** should pray for the power to interpret. For if I **pray in a tongue**, my spirit prays but my mind is unfruitful. (1 Cor. 14:13–14)

And do not forbid **speaking in tongues**. (1 Cor. 14:39)

This charge I commit to you, Timothy, my son, in accordance with the **prophetic utterances** which pointed to you, that inspired by them you may wage the good warfare. (1 Tim. 1:18)

Do not neglect the gift you have, which was given you by **prophetic utterance** when the council of elders laid heir hands upon you. (1 Tim. 4:14)

Healing

For I am the Lord, your **healer**. (Exod. 15:26)

And I will take sickness away from the midst of you. (Exod. 23:25)

And the Lord will take away from you all sickness. (Deut. 7:15)

See now that I, even I, am He, and there is no god beside Me; I kill and I make alive; I wound and **I heal**. (Deut. 32:39)

I have heard your prayer, I have seen your tears; behold, I will **heal** you. (2 Kings 20:5)

O Lord my God, I cried to Thee for help, and Thou hast **healed** me. (Ps. 30:2)

Many are the afflictions of the righteous; but the Lord delivers him out of them all. (Ps. 34:19)

Bless the Lord, O my soul; and **all that is within me**, bless His holy name! Bless the Lord, O my soul, and forget not all His benefits, who forgives all your iniquity, who **heals** all your diseases. (Ps. 103:1–3)

He sent forth His word, and **healed** them. (Ps. 107:20)

Upon Him was the chastisement that made us whole, and with His stripes we are **healed**. (Isa. 53:5)

Therefore confess your sins to one another, and pray for one another, that you may be **healed**. (James 5:16)

By His wounds you have been **healed**. (1 Pet. 2:24)

For the eyes of the Lord are upon the righteous, and His ears are open to their prayer. (1 Pet. 3:12)

Beloved, I pray that all may go well with you and that you may be in **health**. (3 John 2)

Specific Healing Scriptures

Arthritis/Bones

And you have strengthened the **weak hands**. Your words have upheld him who was stumbling, and you have made firm the **feeble knees**. (Job 4:3–4)

Thou didst clothe me with skin and flesh, and knit me together with **bones** and **sinews**. (Job 10:11)

Be gracious to me, O Lord, for I am languishing; O Lord, heal me, for my **bones** are troubled. (Ps. 6:2)

For Thou hast delivered my soul from death, yea, my **feet** from falling, that I may walk before God in the light of life. (Ps. 56:13)

Be not wise in your own eyes; fear the Lord, and turn away from evil. It will be **healing** to your flesh and refreshment to your **bones**. (Prov. 3:7–8)

But they who wait for the Lord shall renew their strength, they shall mount up with wings like eagles, they shall **run** and not be weary, they **shall walk** and not faint. (Isa. 40:31)

And the Lord will guide you continually, and satisfy your desire with good things, and make your **bones** strong. (Isa. 58:11)

For I will restore health to you, and your wounds I will **heal**. (Jer. 30:17)

For the word of the Lord is living and active, sharper than any two-edged sword, piercing to the division of soul and spirit, of **joints** and **marrow**, and discerning the thoughts and intentions of the heart. (Heb. 4:12)

Therefore lift your **drooping hands** and strengthen your **weak knees**, and make straight paths for your **feet,** so that what is lame may not be put out of joint but rather be **healed**. (Heb. 12:12–13)

Allergies/Asthma/Colds

Why are you cast down, O my soul, and why are you disquieted within me? Hope in God; for I shall again praise Him, my help and my God. (Ps. 42:11)

For He will deliver you from the snare of the fowler and from the deadly pestilence. (Ps. 91:3)

Thou didst hear my plea, do not close Thine ear to my cry for help. (Lam. 3:56)

Since He Himself gives to all men life and breath and everything. (Acts 17:25)

Cancer/Diseases

The Lord sustains him on his sickbed; in his illness Thou **healest** all his infirmities. (Ps. 41:3)

For He will deliver you from the snare of the fowler and from the deadly pestilence. (Ps. 91:3)

Who forgives all your iniquity, who **heals** all your diseases. (Ps. 103:3)

Look on my affliction and deliver me, for I do not forget Thy law. (Ps. 119:153)

Though I walk in the midst of trouble, Thou dost preserve my life. (Ps. 138:7)

My son, be attentive to My words; incline your ear to My sayings. Let them not escape from your sight; keep them within your heart. For they are life to him who finds them, and **healing** to all his **flesh**. (Prov. 4:20–22)

Peace, peace, to the far and to the near, says the Lord; and I will **heal** him. (Isa. 57:19)

Heal me, O Lord, and I shall be **healed**; save me, and I shall be saved. (Jer. 17:14)

Whoever says to this mountain, Be taken up and cast into the sea, and does not doubt in his heart, but believes that what he says will come to pass, it will be done for him. Therefore, I tell you, whatever you ask in prayer, believe that you have received it, and it will be yours. (Mark 11:23–24)

Is any among you sick? Let him call for the elders of the church, and let them pray over him, anointing him with oil in the name of the Lord;

and the prayer of faith will save the sick man, and the Lord will raise him up. (James 5:14)

Heart

Relieve the troubles of my **heart**, and bring me out of my distresses. (Ps. 25:17)

My flesh and my **heart** may fail, but God is the strength of my **heart** and my portion forever. (Ps. 73:26)

Keep your **heart** with all vigilance; for from it flow the springs of life. (Prov. 4:23)

A cheerful **heart** is a good medicine, but a downcast spirit dries up the bones. (Prov. 17:22)

He gives power to the faint, and to him who has no might He increases strength. (Isa. 40:29)

Heart

But from there you will seek the Lord your God, and you will find Him; if you search after Him with all your **heart** and with all your soul. (Deut. 4:29)

Know therefore this day, and lay it your **heart**, that the Lord is God in heaven above and on the earth beneath; there is no other. (Deut. 4:39)

Circumcise therefore the foreskin of your **heart**, and be no longer stubborn. (Deut. 10:16)

Take heed lest your **heart** be deceived, and you turn aside and serve other gods and worship them, You shall therefore lay up these words of mine in your **heart** and in your soul. (Deut. 11:16, 18)

And it shall be with him, and he shall read in it all the days of his life, that he may learn to fear the Lord his God, by keeping all the words of this law and these statutes, and doing them, that his **heart** may not be lifted up above his brethren, and that he may not turn aside from the commandment, either to the right hand or to the left. (Deut. 17:19–20)

O Lord, God of Israel, there is no God like Thee, in heaven above or on earth beneath, keeping covenant and showing steadfast love to Thy servants who walk before Thee with all their **heart**. (1 Kings 8:23)

Then hear thou in heaven Thy dwelling place, and forgive, and act, and render to each whose **heart** Thou knowest, according to all his ways (for Thou, Thou only, knowest the **hearts** of all the children of men). (1 Kings 8:39)

That He may incline our **hearts** to Him, to walk in all His ways, and to keep His commandments, His statutes, and His ordinances, Let your **heart** therefore be wholly true to the Lord our God. (1 Kings 8:58, 61)

Answer me, O Lord, answer me, that this people may know that Thou, O Lord, art God, and that Thou has turned their **hearts** back. (1 Kings 18:37)

I will give thanks to the Lord with my whole **heart**; I will tell of all Thy wonderful deeds. (Ps. 9:1)

Keep your **heart** with all vigilance; for from it flow the springs of life. (Prov. 4:23)

A glad **heart** makes a cheerful countenance, but by sorrow of **heart** the spirit is broken. (Prov. 15:13)

Return to me with all your **heart**, with fasting, with weeping, and with mourning; and rend your **hearts** and not your garments. (Joel 2:12–13)

For where your treasure is, there will your **heart** be also. (Matt. 6:21)

In return—I speak as to children—widen your **hearts** also. (2 Cor. 6:13)

Therefore I was provoked with that generation, and said, They always go astray in their **hearts**; they have not known My ways. (Heb. 3:10)

I will put My laws into their minds, and write them on their **hearts**. (Heb. 8:10)

Let us draw near with a true **heart** in full assurance of faith, with our **hearts** sprinkled clean from an evil conscience and our bodies washed with pure water. (Heb. 10:22)

You also be patient, establish your **hearts,** for the coming of the Lord is at hand. (James 5:8)

Having purified your souls by your obedience to the truth for a sincere love of the brethren, love one another earnestly from the **heart.** (1 Pet. 1:22)

But let it be the hidden person of the **heart** with the imperishable jewel of a gentle and quiet spirit, which in God's sight is very precious. Finally, all of you, have unity of spirit, sympathy, love of the brethren, a tender **heart** and a humble mind. (1 Pet. 3:4, 8)

But in your **hearts** reverence Christ as Lord. (1 Pet. 3:15)

Beloved, if our **hearts** do not condemn us, we have confidence before God. (1 John 3:21)

And all the churches shall know that I am He who searches mind and **heart,** and I will give to each of you as your works deserve. (Rev. 2:23)

Holiness / Personal Conduct

Who is like Thee, O Lord, among the gods? Who is like Thee, majestic in **holiness.** (Exod. 15:11)

Consecrate yourselves therefore, and be **holy,** for I am holy. you shall therefore be **holy,** for I am holy. (Lev. 11:44–45)

You shall be **holy**; for I the Lord your God am holy. (Lev. 19:2)

And you shall observe all my statutes and all my ordinances, and do them: I am the Lord. (Lev. 19:37)

Consecrate yourselves therefore, and be **holy**; for I am the Lord your God. (Lev. 20:7)

You shall be **holy** to me; for I the Lord am holy, and have separated you from the peoples, that you should be mine. (Lev. 20:26)

So you shall remember and do all my commandments, and be **holy** to your God. (Num. 15:40)

And you shall do what is **right** and **good** in the sight of the Lord, that it may go well with you. (Deut. 6:18)

What does the Lord your God require of you, but to **fear the Lord** your God, to walk in all His ways, to love Him, to serve the Lord your God with all your heart and with all your soul, and to keep the commandments and statutes of the Lord. (Deut. 10:12–13)

You shall be **blameless** before the Lord your God. (Deut. 18:13)

I was **blameless** before Him, and I kept myself from guilt. Therefore the Lord has recompensed me according to my **righteousness**, according to my cleanness in His sight. (2 Sam. 22:24–25)

Do not be deceived; "Bad company ruins **good morals**." (1 Cor. 15:33)

Even as He chose us in Him before the foundation of the world, that we should be **holy and blameless** before Him. (Eph. 1:4)

For we are His workmanship, created in Christ Jesus for **good works**. (Eph. 2:10)

And be renewed in the spirit of your minds, and put on the new nature, created after the likeness of God in **true righteousness** and **holiness**. (Eph. 4:23–24)

To lead a life **worthy** of God, who calls you into His own kingdom and glory. (1 Thess. 2:12)

And may the Lord make you increase and abound in love to one another and to all men, so that He may establish your hearts **unblamable** in holiness before our God and Father. (1 Thess. 3:12–13)

That we may lead a quiet and peaceable life, **godly** and **respectful** in every way. (1 Tim. 2:2)

Train yourself in **godliness**; godliness is of value in every way. (1 Tim. 4:7–8)

Keep yourself **pure**. (1 Tim. 5:22)

Aim at **righteousness**, **godliness**, faith, love, steadfastness, gentleness. (1 Tim. 11:11)

Do your best to present yourself to God as one **approved**, a workman who has no need to be ashamed, rightly handling the word of truth. (2 Tim. 2:15)

If any one **purifies** himself from what is ignoble, then he will be a vessel for noble use, **consecrated**, and useful to the master of the house, ready for any good work. And the Lord's servant must not be quarrelsome but **kindly** to every one, an apt teacher, forbearing, correcting his opponents with gentleness. (2 Tim. 2:21, 24)

Training us to renounce irreligion and worldly passions, and to live sober, upright, and **godly** lives in this world. (Titus 2:12)

Remind them to be **submissive** to rulers and authorities, to be **obedient**, to be ready for any honest work, to speak evil of no one, to avoid quarreling, to be **gentle**, and to show perfect courtesy toward all men, so that those who have believed in God may be careful to apply themselves to **good deeds**. (Titus 3:1–2, 8)

But He disciplines us for our good, that we may share His holiness. Strive for peace with all men, and for the **holiness** without which no one will see the Lord. (Heb. 12:10, 14)

Do not neglect to do good and to **share** what you have, for such sacrifices are pleasing to God. (Heb. 13:16)

Religion that is **pure** and **undefiled** before God and the Father is this: to visit orphans and widows in their affliction, and to keep oneself **unstained** from the world. (James 1:27)

Humble yourselves before the Lord and He will exalt you. (James 4:10)

But as He who called you is holy, be **holy** yourselves in all your conduct; since it is written, "You shall be holy, for I am holy." (1 Pet. 1:15–16)

And like living stones be yourselves built into a spiritual house, to be a **holy** priesthood. (1 Pet. 2:5)

Clothe yourselves all of you, with **humility** toward one another, for God opposes the proud, but gives grace to the humble. (1 Pet. 5:5)

His divine power has granted to us all things that pertain to life and godliness, through the knowledge of Him who called us to His own glory and excellence, For this very reason make every effort to supplement our faith with **virtue,** and virtue with **knowledge**, and knowledge with **self-control**, and self-control with **steadfastness,** and steadfastness with **godliness**, and godliness with **brotherly affection**, and brotherly affection with **love**. (2 Pet. 1:3, 5–7)

What sort of persons ought you to be in lives of **holiness** and **godliness,** Therefore, beloved, since you wait for these, be zealous to be found by Him **without spot or blemish**, and at peace. (2 Pet. 3:11, 14)

Holy Spirit / Spirit of God

And the **Spirit of God** was moving over the face of the waters. (Gen. 1:2)

Can we find such a man as this, in whom is the **Spirit of God**? (Gen. 41:38)

And He has filled him with the **Spirit of God**. (Exod. 35:31)

Then the Lord came down in the cloud and spoke to him, and took some of the **spirit** that was upon him and put it upon the seventy elders; and when the **spirit** rested upon them, they prophesied. (Num. 11:25)

And Balaam lifted up his eyes, and saw Israel encamping tribe by tribe. And the **Spirit of God** came upon him. (Num. 24:2)

The **Spirit of the Lord** came upon him, and he judged Israel. (Judg. 3:10)

And I will put My **Spirit** within you, and cause you to walk in My statues and be careful to observe My ordinances. (Ezek. 36:27)

And it shall come to pass afterward, that I will pour out My **spirit** on all flesh; your sons and your daughters shall prophesy, your old men shall dream dreams, and your young men shall see visions. Even upon the menservants and maidservants in those days, I will pour out My **spirit**. (Joel 2:28–29)

He will baptize you with the **Holy Spirit** and with fire. (Matt. 3:11)

Go therefore and make disciples of all nations, baptizing them in the name of the

Father and of the Son and of the **Holy Spirit**. (Matt. 28:19)

And I will pray the Father, and He will give you another **Counselor**, to be with you for ever, even the **Spirit of Truth**, whom the world cannot receive, because it neither sees Him nor knows Him; you know Him for He dwells with you, and will be in you. (John 14:16)

When the **Spirit of Truth** comes, He will guide you into all the truth. (John 16:13)

For all who are led by the **Spirit of God** are sons of God. (Rom. 8:14)

It is the **Spirit** himself bearing witness with our spirit that we are children of God. (Rom. 8:16)

But, as it is written, What no eye has seen nor ear heard, nor the heart of man conceived, what God has prepared for those who love Him, God has revealed to us through the **Spirit**. For the **Spirit** searches everything, even the depths of God. For what person knows a man's thoughts except the spirit of the man which is in him? So also no one comprehends the thoughts of God except the **Spirit of God**. (1 Cor. 2:9–11)

For by one **Spirit** we were all baptized into one body-Jews or Greeks, slaves or free-and all were made to drink of one **Spirit**. (1 Cor. 12:13)

Now the Lord is the **Spirit,** and where the **Spirit of the Lord** is, there is freedom. (2 Cor. 3:17)

In Him you also, who have heard the word of truth and have believed in Him were sealed with the promised **Holy Spirit**. (Eph. 1:13)

Guard the truth that has been entrusted to you by the **Holy Spirit** who dwells within us. (2 Tim. 1:14)

He saved us, by the washing of regeneration and renewal in the **Holy Spirit**. (Titus 3:5)

While God also bore witness by signs and wonders and various miracles and by gifts of the **Holy Spirit** distributed according to His own will. (Heb. 2:4)

And the **Holy Spirit** also bears witness to us. (Heb. 10:15)

Because no prophesy ever came by the impulse of man, but men moved by the **Holy Spirit** spoke from God. (2 Pet. 1:21)

But you have been anointed by the **Holy One**. (1 John 2:20)

And by this we know that He abides in us, by the **Spirit** which He has given us. (1 John 3:24)

For He who is in you is greater than he who is in the world. By this we know that we abide in Him and He in us, because He has given us of His own **Spirit**. (1 John 4:4, 13)

And the **Spirit** is the witness, because the **Spirit** is the truth. There are three witnesses, the

Spirit, the water, and the blood; and these three agree. (1 John 5:7, 8)

But you, beloved, build yourselves up on your most holy faith; pray in the **Holy Spirit**. (Jude 20)

Hope

We have this as a sure and steadfast anchor of the soul, a **hope** that enters into the inner shrine behind the curtain. (Heb. 6:19)

For the law made nothing perfect; on the other hand, a better **hope** is introduced, through which we draw near to God. (Heb. 7:19)

Let us hold fast the confession of our **hope** without wavering, for He who promised is faithful. (Heb. 10:23)

Idols

You shall have no other gods before Me. You shall not make for yourself a **graven image**, you shall not bow down to them or serve them. (Exod. 20:3–5)

You shall not make **gods of silver** to be with Me, nor shall you make for yourselves **gods of gold**. (Exod. 20:23)

You shall not permit a **sorceress** to live. (Exod. 22:18)

You shall not bow down to their gods, nor serve them. (Exod. 23:24)

For you shall worship no other god, for the Lord, whose name is Jealous, is a jealous God. (Exod. 34:14)

Do not turn to **idols** or make for yourselves **molten gods**. (Lev. 19:4)

You shall not practice **augury** or **witchcraft**. (Lev. 19:26)

Do not turn to **mediums** or **wizards;** do not seek them out. (Lev. 19:31)

If a person turn to **mediums** and **wizards**, playing the harlot after them, I will set My face against that person. (Lev. 20:6)

A man or a woman who is a **medium** or a **wizard** shall be put to death. (Lev. 20:27)

You shall make for yourselves no **idols** and erect no **graven image or pillar**, and you shall not set up a **figured stone** in your land, to bow down to them. (Lev. 26:1)

You shall have no other gods before Me. You shall not make for yourself a **graven image**, you shall not bow down to them or serve them. (Deut. 5:7–9)

The **graven images** of their gods you shall burn with fire; you shall not covet the silver or the gold that is on them, or take it for yourselves, lest you be ensnared by it. (Deut. 7:25–26)

And if you forget the Lord your God and go after **other gods** and serve them and worship them, I solemnly warn you this day that you shall surely perish. (Deut. 8:19)

Take heed lest your heart be deceived, and you turn aside and serve **other gods** and worship them. (Deut. 11:16)

For every abominable thing which the Lord hates they have done for their gods; for they even burn their sons and their daughters in the fire to their gods. (Deut. 12:31)

You shall not listen to the words of that **prophet** or to that **dreamer of dreams**. (Deut. 13:3)

You shall not plant any tree as an **Asherah** beside the altar of the Lord your God which you shall make. And you shall not set up a **pillar**, which the Lord your God hates. (Deut. 16:21–22)

There shall not be found among you any one who burns his son or his daughter as an **offering**, any one who practices **divination**, a **soothsayer**, or an **augur**, or a **sorcerer**, or a **charmer**, or a **medium**, or a **wizard**, or a **necromancer**. (Deut. 18:10–11)

Cursed be the man who makes a **graven or molten image**, an abomination to the Lord. (Deut. 27:15)

If you forsake the Lord and serve **foreign gods**, then He will turn and do you harm, and consume you. (Josh. 24:20)

You shall not fear other gods or bow yourselves to them or serve them or sacrifice to them. (2 Kings 17:35)

And he burned his son as an offering, and practiced **soothsaying** and **augury,** and dealt with **mediums** and with **wizards**. He did much evil in the sight of the Lord, provoking Him to anger. (2 Kings 21:6)

For all the gods of the peoples are **idols**. (1 Chron. 16:26)

Thou hatest those who pay regard to **vain idols**. (Ps. 31:6)

And when they say to you, "consult the **mediums** and the **wizards** who chirp and mutter," should not a people consult their God? Should they consult the dead on behalf of the living? (Isa. 8:19)

And the spirit of the Egyptians within them will be emptied out, and I will confound their plans; and they will consult the **idols** and the **sorcerers**, and the **mediums** and the **wizards**. (Isa. 19:3)

All who make **idols** are nothing, and the things they delight in do not profit. (Isa. 44:9)

Stand fast in your **enchantments** and your many **sorceries**, with which you have labored from your youth; perhaps you may be able to succeed, perhaps you may inspire terror. You are wearied with your many counsels; let them stand forth and save you, those **who divide the heavens**, **who gaze** at **the stars**, who at the new moons predict what shall befall you. Behold, they are like stubble, the fire consumes them. (Isa. 47:12–14)

And I will cut off **sorceries** from your hand, and you shall have no more **soothsayers**. (Micah 5:12)

Do not be deceived; neither the immoral, nor **idolators**, nor **adulterers,** nor sexual perverts, nor thieves, nor the greedy, nor drunkards, nor revilers, nor robbers will inherit the kingdom of God. (1 Cor. 6:9–10)

Now the works of the flesh are plain: fornication, impurity, licentiousness, **idolatry, sorcery**, enmity, strife, jealousy, anger, selfishness, dissension, party spirit, envy, drunkenness, carousing and the like. I warn you, as I warned you before, that those who do such things shall not inherit the kingdom of God. (Gal. 5:19–21)

Have nothing to do with godless and **silly myths**. (1 Tim. 4:7)

Little children, keep yourselves from **idols**. (1 John 5:21)

But as for the cowardly, the faithless, the polluted, as for murderers, fornicators, **sorcerers, idolaters,** and all liars, their lot shall be in the lake that burns with fire and sulphur, which is the second death. (Rev. 21:8)

Outside are the dogs and **sorcerers** and fornicators and murderers and **idolaters**, and every one who loves and **practices falsehood**. (Rev. 22:15)

Intercession

He saw that there was no man, and wondered that there was no one to **intervene**; then His own arm brought Him victory, and His righteousness upheld Him. (Isa. 59:16)

You have not **gone up into the breaches**, or built up a wall for the house of Israel, that it might stand in battle in the day of the Lord. (Ezek. 13:5)

And I sought for a man among them who should build up the wall and **stand in the breach** before Me for the land. (Ezek. 22:30)

Likewise the Spirit helps us in our weakness; for we do not know how to pray as we ought, but the Spirit himself **intercedes** for us with sighs too deep for words. (Rom. 8:26–27)

He is able for all time to save those who draw near to God through Him since He always lives to make **intercession** for them. (Heb. 7:25)

Joy

Thy words were found, and I ate them, and Thy words became to me a **joy** and the delight of my heart. (Jer. 15:16)

You have been faithful over a little, I will set you over much; enter into the **joy** of your master. (Matt. 25:21)

Be not afraid; for behold, I bring you good news of a great **joy** which will come to all the people. (Luke 2:10)

Count it all **joy**, my brethren, when you meet various trials, for you know that the testing of your faith produces steadfastness. (James 1:2)

For the **joy** of the Lord is your strength. (Neh. 8:10)

Thou hast put more **joy** in my heart than they have when their grain and wine abound. (Ps. 4:7)

Then I will go to the altar of God, to God my exceeding **joy**. (Ps. 43:4)

Restore to me the **joy** of Thy salvation, and uphold me with a willing spirit. (Ps. 51:12)

My heart and flesh sing for **joy** to the living God. (Ps. 84:2)

Light dawns for the righteous, and **joy** for the upright in heart. (Ps. 97:11)

May those who sow in tears reap with shouts of **joy**! (Ps. 126:5)

For you shall go out in **joy**, and be led forth in peace. (Isa. 55:12)

Judgment

But I will bring **judgment** on the nation which they serve. (Gen. 15:14)

Shall not the **Judge** of all the earth do right? (Gen. 18:25)

And I will redeem you with an outstretched arm and with great acts of **judgment**. (Exod. 6:6)

Keeping steadfast love for thousands, forgiving iniquity and transgression and sin, but who will by no means clear the guilty, visiting the iniquity of the fathers upon the children and the children's children, to the third and the fourth generation. (Exod. 34:7)

And he shall pay as the **judges** determine. (Exod. 21:22)

You shall do no injustice in **judgment**; you shall not be partial to the poor or defer to the great, but in righteousness shall you **judge** your neighbor. You shall do no wrong in **judgment**. (Lev. 19:15, 35)

But He will by no means clear the guilty, visiting the iniquity of fathers upon children, upon the third and upon the fourth generation. (Num. 14:18)

You shall not be partial in **judgment**; you shall not be afraid of the face of man, for the **judgment** is God's. (Deut. 1:17)

For the Lord your God is God of gods and Lord of lords, who is not partial and takes no bribe. He executes **justice** for the fatherless and the widow, and loves the sojourner. (Deut. 10:17–18)

You shall appoint judges and officers in all your towns which the Lord your God gives you, and they shall **judge** the people with righteous **judgment**. You shall not pervert justice; you shall not show partiality; and you shall not take a bribe, for a bribe blinds the eyes of the wise and subverts the cause of the righteous. Justice, and only justice, you shall follow. (Deut. 16:18–20)

The Rock, His work is perfect; for all His ways are **justice**. (Deut. 32:4)

Vengeance is mine, and recompense, for the day of their calamity is at hand, and their doom comes swiftly. (Deut. 32:35)

For the Lord is a God of knowledge, and by Him actions are weighed. (1 Sam. 2:3)

I will **judge** each of you according to his ways. (Ezek. 33:20)

Judge not, that you be not **judged**. For with the **judgment** you pronounce you will be **judged**, and the measure you give will be the measure you get. (Matt. 7:1–2)

I tell you, on the day of **judgment** men will render account for every careless word they utter; for by your words you will be justified, and by your words you will be condemned. (Matt. 12:36)

Do not **judge** by appearances, but **judge** with right **judgment**. (John 7:24)

You **judge** according to the flesh, I **judge** no one. Yet even if I do **judge**, my **judgment** is true, for it is not I alone that **judge,** but I and He who sent me. (John 8:15–16)

When you **judge** another; for in passing **judgment** upon him you condemn yourself, because you, the **judge**, are doing the very same things. (Rom. 2:1)

Then let us no more pass **judgment** on one another, but rather decide never to put a stumbling block or hindrance in the way of a brother. (Rom. 14:13)

For we must all appear before the **judgment** seat of Christ, so that each one may receive good or evil, according to what he has done in the body. (2 Cor. 5:10)

For if we sin deliberately after receiving the knowledge of the truth, there no longer remains a sacrifice for sins, but a fearful prospect of **judgment,** and a fury of fire which will consume the adversaries. For we know Him who said, "Vengeance is mine, I will repay." (Heb. 10:26–27, 30)

My brethren, show no partiality as you hold the faith of our Lord Jesus Christ the

Lord of glory. Have you not made distinctions among yourselves, and become **judges** with evil thoughts? But if you show partiality, you commit sin, So speak and so act as those who are to be **judged** under the law of liberty. For **judgment** is without mercy to one who has shown no mercy; yet mercy triumphs over **judgment**. (James 2:1, 4, 9, 12–13)

Do not speak evil against one another, brethren. He that speaks evil against a brother or **judges** his brother speaks evil against the law and **judges** the law. But if you **judge** the law, you are not a doer of the law but a **judge**. There is one lawgiver and **judge,** He who is able to save and to destroy. But who are you that you **judge** your neighbor? (James 4:11–12)

In this is love perfected with us, that we may have confidence for the day of **judgment**. (1 John 4:17)

Behold, the Lord came with His holy myriads, to execute **judgment** on all. (Jude 14, 15)

And He said with a loud voice, Fear God and give Him glory, for the hour of His **judgment** has come. (Rev. 14:7)

And I heard the altar cry, Yea, Lord God the Almighty, true and just are Thy **judgments**! (Rev. 16:7)

For His **judgments** are true and just. (Rev. 19:2)

Kindness

But happy is he who is **kind** to the poor. (Prov. 14:21)

She opens her hand to the poor, and reaches out her hands to the needy. (Prov. 31:20)

Outdo one another in showing honor. Contribute to the needs of the saints, practice **hospitality**. (Rom. 12:10, 13)

Love is patient and **kind**. (1 Cor. 13:4)

And be **kind** to one another, tenderhearted. (Eph. 4:32)

Put on then, as God's chosen ones, holy and beloved, compassion, **kindness,** lowliness, meekness, and patience. (Col. 3:12)

For you have tasted the **kindness** of the Lord. (1 Pet. 2:3)

Lamb's Book of Life

But now, if Thou wilt forgive their sin—and if not, blot me, I pray Thee, out of **Thy book** which Thou hast written. But the Lord said to Moses, Whoever has sinned against Me, him will I blot out of **My book**. (Exod. 32:32–33)

And I ask you also, help these women for they have labored side by side with me in the gospel together with Clement and the rest of my fellow workers, whose names are in the **book of life**. (Phil. 4:3)

Then I said, Lo, I have come to do Thy will O God, as it is written of me in the roll of **the book**. (Heb. 10:7)

I write this to you who believe in the name of the Son of God, that you may know that you have eternal life. (1 John 5:13)

He who conquers shall be clad thus in white garments, and I will not blot his name out of the **book of life**. (Rev. 3:5)

And the dwellers on earth whose names have not been written in the **book of life** from the foundation of the world, will marvel to behold the beast. (Rev. 17:8)

And I saw the dead, great and small, standing before the throne, and books were opened. Also another book was opened, which is the **book of life**. And the dead were judged by what was written in the books, by what they had done. And if any one's name was not found written in the **book of life**, he was thrown into the lake of fire. (Rev. 20:12, 15)

But nothing unclean shall enter it, nor any one who practices abomination or falsehood, but only those who are written in the **Lamb's book of life**. (Rev. 21:27)

Law

There shall be one **law** for the native and for the stranger who sojourns among you. (Exod. 12:49)

And it shall be to you as a sign on your hand and as a memorial between your eyes, that the **law** of the Lord may be in your mouth. (Exod. 13:9)

(The Ten Commandments) The **Law** given—You shall have no other gods before Me. You shall not make for yourself a graven image, you shall not bow down to them or serve them; You shall not take the name of the Lord your God in vain; Remember the Sabbath day, to keep it holy. Honor your father and your mother, You shall not kill. You shall not commit adultery. You shall not steal. You shall not bear false witness against your neighbor. You shall not covet your neighbor's house. (Exod. 20:3–17)

If any harm follows, then you shall give life for life, eye for eye, tooth for tooth, hand for hand, foot for foot, burn for burn, wound for wound, stripe for stripe. (Exod. 21:23)

The Lord said to Moses, "Come up to Me on the mountain, and wait there; and I will give you the tables of stone, with the **law** and the commandment, which I have written for your instruction." (Exod. 24:12)

You shall not steal, nor deal falsely, nor lie to one another. You shall keep My Sabbaths and reverence My sanctuary: I am the Lord. (Lev. 19:11, 30)

When a man vows a vow to the Lord, or swears an oath to bind himself by a pledge, he shall not break his word; he shall do according to all that proceeds out of his mouth. (Num. 30:2)

Leaders of Church / Those in Authority

And Aaron your brother shall be your **prophet**. (Exod. 7:1)

And you shall be to Me a kingdom of **priests** and a holy nation. (Exod. 19:6)

Drink no wine nor strong drink, you nor your sons with you, when you go into the tent of meeting, lest you die; it shall be a statute for ever throughout your generations. You are to distinguish between the holy and the common, and between the unclean and the clean. (Lev. 10:9–11)

If there is a **prophet** among you, I the Lord make Myself known to him in a vision, I speak with him in a dream. (Num. 12:6)

You shall have no inheritance in their land, neither shall you have any portion among them; I am your portion and your inheritance among the people. (Num. 18:20)

I will raise up for them a **prophet** like you from among their brethren; and I will put My words in his mouth, and he shall speak to them all that I command him. (Deut. 18:18)

Love

Thou hast led in Thy steadfast **love** the people whom Thou hast redeemed. (Exod. 15:13)

But showing steadfast **love** to thousands of those who love Me and keep My commandments. (Exod. 20:6)

The Lord, the Lord, a God merciful and gracious, slow to anger, and abounding in steadfast **love** and faithfulness. (Exod. 34:6)

But you shall **love** your neighbor as yourself; I am the Lord. (Lev. 19:18)

The Lord is slow to anger, and abounding in steadfast **love**. (Num. 14:18)

Hear, O Israel, The Lord our God is one Lord; and you shall **love** the Lord your God with all your heart, and with all your soul, and with all your might. (Deut. 6:4)

Know therefore that the Lord your God is God, the faithful God who keeps covenant and steadfast **love** with those who **love** Him and keep His commandments. (Deut. 7:9)

What does the Lord your God require of you, but to fear the Lord your God, to walk in all His ways, to **love** Him, to serve the Lord your God with all your heart and with all your soul, yet the Lord set His heart in **love** upon your fathers and chose their descendants after them. (Deut. 10:12, 15)

You shall therefore **love** the Lord your God, and keep His charge. (Deut. 11:1)

And the Lord your God will circumcise your heart and the heart of your offspring, so that you will **love** the Lord your God with all your heart and with all your soul, that you may live. (Deut. 30:6)

Take good heed to yourselves, therefore, to **love** the Lord your God. (Josh. 23:11)

There is no God like Thee, in heaven above or on earth beneath, keeping covenant and showing steadfast **love** to Thy servants who walk before Thee with all their heart. (1 Kings 8:23)

But steadfast **love** surrounds him who trusts in the Lord. (Ps. 32:10)

For I am sure that neither death, nor life, nor angels, nor principalities, nor things present, nor things to come, nor powers, nor height, nor depth, nor anything else in all creation, will be able to separate us from the **love** of God in Christ Jesus our Lord. (Rom. 8:38)

Let **love** be genuine; **love** one another with brotherly affection. (Rom. 12:9, 10)

Owe no one anything, except to **love** one another; for he who **loves** his neighbor has fulfilled the law. (Rom. 13:8)

Love is patient and kind; **love** is not jealous or boastful; it is not arrogant or rude. **Love**

does not insist on its own way; it is not irritable or resentful; it does not rejoice at wrong, but rejoices in the right. **Love** bears all things, believes all things, hopes all things, endures all things. **Love** never ends. (1 Cor. 13:4–8)

But through **love** be servants of one another. You shall **love** your neighbor as yourself. (Gal. 5:13–14)

And above all these, put on **love**, which binds everything together in perfect harmony. (Col. 3:14)

Above all hold unfailing your **love** for one another, since **love** covers a multitude of sins. (1 Pet. 4:8)

Greet one another with the kiss of **love**. (1 Pet. 5:14)

For this is the message which you have heard from the beginning, that we should **love** one another, Little children, let us not **love** in word or speech but in deed and in truth. (1 John 3:11, 18)

And this is His commandment, that we should believe in the name of His Son Jesus Christ and **love** one another. (1 John 3:23)

Beloved, let us **love** one another; for **love** is of God, and he who **loves** is born of God and knows God. He who does not love does not know God; for God is **love**. In this the **love** of God was made manifest among us, that God sent His only Son into the world, so that we might live through Him. In this is **love**, not that we **loved** God but that He **loved** us and sent His Son to be the expiation for our sins. Beloved, if God so **loved** us, we also ought to **love** one another. No man has ever seen God; if we **love** one another, God abides in us and His **love** is perfected in us. (1 John 4:7–12)

There is no fear in **love,** but perfect **love** casts out fear. We **love,** because He first **loved** us. (1 John 4:18, 19)

And this is **love**, that we follow His commandments; this is the commandment, as you have heard from the beginning, that you follow **love**. (2 John 6)

Markings in Flesh

You shall not round off the hair on your temples or mar the edges of your beard. You shall not make any **cuttings in your flesh** on account of the dead or **tattoo** any marks upon you: I am the Lord. (Lev. 19:27–28)

They shall not make tonsures upon their heads, nor shave off the edges of their beards, nor make any **cuttings** in their **flesh**. (Lev. 21:5)

You are the sons of the Lord your God; you shall not **cut** yourselves or make any **baldness** on your foreheads for the dead. (Deut. 14:1)

Marriage

Therefore a man leaves his father and his mother and cleaves to his wife, and they become **one flesh**. (Gen. 2:24)

Let your fountain be blessed, and rejoice in the **wife of your youth**, a lovely hind, a graceful doe. Let her affection fill you at all times with delight, be infatuated always with her love. (Prov. 5:18–19)

A good wife is the crown of her husband, but she who brings shame is like rottenness in his bones. (Prov. 12:4)

He who finds a wife finds a good thing, and obtains favor from the Lord. (Prov. 18:22)

Enjoy life with the wife whom you love, all the days of your vain life. (Eccles. 9:9)

But from the beginning of creation, God made them male and female. For this reason a man shall leave his father and mother and be joined to his wife, and the two shall become **one flesh**. So they are no longer two but one flesh. What therefore God has joined together, let not man put asunder. (Mark 10:6–9)

Each man should have his own wife and each woman should have her own husband. The husband should give to his wife her conjugal rights, and likewise the wife to her husband. (1 Cor. 7:2, 3)

Do not be mis-mated with unbelievers. Therefore come out from them, and be separate from them, says the Lord. (2 Cor. 6:14, 17)

Wives, be subject to your husbands, Husbands, love your wives, For this reason a man shall leave his father and mother and be joined to his wife, and the two shall become **one flesh**. However, let each one of you love his wife as himself, and let the wife see that she respects her husband. (Eph. 5:22, 25, 31, 33)

Wives, be subject to your husbands, as is fitting in the Lord. **Husbands**, love your wives, and do not be harsh with them. (Col. 3:18–19)

That each one of you know how to take a **wife** for himself in holiness and honor, not in the passion of lust like heathen who do not know God. (1 Thess. 4:4–5)

And so train the young women to love their **husbands** and children, to be sensible, chaste, domestic, kind, and submissive to their **husbands**. (Titus 2:4, 5)

Let **marriage** be held in honor among all, and let the marriage bed be undefiled. (Heb. 13:4)

Likewise you **wives**, be submissive to your **husbands** so that some, though they do not obey the word, may be won without a word by the behavior of their **wives**. Likewise you **husbands**, live considerately with your **wives**, bestowing honor on the woman as the weaker sex. (1 Pet. 3:1, 7)

Mercy

And I will be gracious to whom I will be gracious, and will show **mercy** on whom I will show **mercy**. (Exod. 33:19)

The Lord, the Lord, a God **merciful** and gracious, slow to anger, and abounding in steadfast love and faithfulness. (Exod. 34:6)

And His **mercy** is on those who fear Him from generation to generation. (Luke 1:50)

For I will be **merciful** toward their iniquities, and I will remember their sins no more. (Heb. 8:12)

You have heard of the steadfastness of Job, and you have seen the purpose of the Lord, how the Lord is compassionate and **merciful**. (James 5:11)

Money

If you lend **money** to any of my people with you who is poor, you shall not be to him as a creditor, and you shall not exact interest from him. (Exod. 22:25)

Take no interest from him or increase, but fear your God; that your brother may live beside you. You shall not lend him your **money** at interest, nor give him your food for profit. (Lev. 25:36–37)

You shall remember the Lord your God, for it is He who gives you power to get **wealth**. (Deut. 8:18)

For the Lord your God will bless you, as He promised you, and you shall lend to many nations, but you shall not borrow. (Deut. 15:6)

You shall not lend upon interest to your brother, interest on **money**, interest on victuals, interest on anything that is lent for interest. (Deut. 23:19)

No one can serve two masters; for either he will hate the one and love the other, or he will be devoted to the one and despise the other. You cannot serve God and **mammon**. (Matt. 6:24)

Obedience

Has the Lord as great delight in burnt offerings and sacrifices, as in **obeying** the voice of the Lord? Behold, to **obey** is better than sacrifice. (1 Sam. 15:22)

If you will walk in My statutes and **obey** My ordinances and keep all My commandments and walk in them, then I will establish My word with you. (1 Kings 6:12)

If you are willing and **obedient**, you shall eat the good of the land. (Isa. 1:19)

We must **obey** God rather than men. (Acts 5:29)

Oppression

And now, behold, the cry of the people of Israel has come to Me, and I have seen the **oppression** with which the Egyptians oppress them. (Exod. 3:9)

You shall not wrong a stranger or **oppress** him. (Exod. 22:21)

You shall not **oppress** a stranger; you know the heart of a stranger. (Exod. 23:9)

You shall not **oppress** your neighbor or rob him. (Lev. 19:13)

You shall not **oppress** a hired servant who is poor and needy. (Deut. 24:14)

The Lord is a stronghold for the **oppressed**, a stronghold in times of trouble. (Ps. 9:9)

Be surety for Thy servant for good; let not the godless **oppress** me. (Ps. 119:122)

Redeem me from man's **oppression,** that I may keep Thy precepts. (Ps. 119:134)

Surely **oppression** makes the wise man foolish. (Eccles. 7:7)

How God anointed Jesus of Nazareth with the Holy Spirit and with power; how He went about doing good and healing all that were **oppressed** by the devil. (Acts 10:38)

Overcoming

Let the redeemed of the Lord say so, whom He has **redeemed** from trouble. (Ps. 107:2)

Therefore, we are now **justified** by His blood, much more shall we be saved by Him from the wrath of God. (Rom. 5:9)

For our sake He made Him to be sin who knew no sin, so that in Him we might become the righteousness of God. (2 Cor. 5:21)

In Him we have **redemption** through His blood, the forgiveness of sins, according to the riches of His grace. (Eph. 1:7)

Him that **overcometh** will I make a pillar in the temple of my God. (Rev. 3:12)

To him that **overcometh** will I grant to sit with Me on My throne. (Rev. 3:21)

Patience

He who is **slow to anger** is better than the mighty, and he who rules his spirit than he who takes a city. (Prov. 16:32)

They are those who, hearing the word, hold it fast in an honest and good heart, and bring forth fruit with **patience**. (Luke 8:15)

By your **endurance** you will gain your lives. (Luke 21:19)

To those who by **patience** in well doing seek for glory and honor and immortality, He will give eternal life. (Rom. 2:7)

For you know that the testing of your faith produces **steadfastness** (patience), and let **steadfastness** have its full effect that you may be perfect and complete, lacking in nothing. (James 1:3–4)

Be **patient** until the coming of the Lord. (James 5:7)

Peace

But the Lord said to him, "**Peace** be to you; do not fear," Then Gideon built an altar there to the Lord, and called it, The Lord is **peace**. (Judg. 6:23, 24)

Go in **peace**, and the God of Israel grant your petition which you have made to Him. (1 Sam. 1:17)

May the Lord bless His people with **peace**! (Ps. 29:11)

Thou dost keep him in perfect **peace,** whose mind is stayed on Thee, because he trusts in Thee. (Isa. 26:3)

O Lord, Thou wilt ordain **peace** for us. (Isa. 26:12)

And the effect of righteousness will be **peace**, My people will abide in a **peaceful** habitation, in secure dwellings, and in quiet resting places. (Isa. 32:17, 18)

There is no **peace**, says my God, for the wicked. (Isa. 57:21)

And be at **peace** with one another. (Mark 9:50)

For God is not a God of confusion but of **peace**. (1 Cor. 14:33)

For He is our **peace,** who has made us both one, and has broken down the dividing wall of hostility. (Eph. 2:14)

And the **peace** of God, which passes all understanding, will keep your hearts and your minds in Christ Jesus. (Phil. 4:7)

What you have learned and received and heard and seen in Me, do; and the God of **peace** will be with you. (Phil. 4:9)

And let the **peace** of Christ rule in your hearts. (Col. 3:15)

Now may the Lord of **peace** Himself give you **peace** at all times in all ways. (2 Thess. 3:16)

Strive for **peace** with all men, and for the holiness without which no one will see the Lord. (Heb. 12:14)

And the harvest of righteousness is sown in **peace** by those who make **peace**. (James 3:18)

Peace to all of you that are in Christ. (1 Pet. 5:14)

May grace and **peace** be multiplied to you in the knowledge of God and of Jesus our Lord. (2 Pet. 1:2)

Therefore, beloved, since you wait for these, be zealous to be found by Him without spot or blemish, and at **peace**. (2 Pet. 3:14)

Popular Clichés/Scriptures

Spoken over the years and documentation of where they are in the Bible:

Aaronic benediction (similar to Irish blessing).

The Lord bless you and keep you: The Lord make His face to shine upon you, and be gracious to you; The Lord lift up His countenance upon you, and give you peace. (Num. 6:24–26)

A merry heart doeth good like a medicine.

A cheerful heart is a good medicine. (Prov. 17:22)

And the two shall be one flesh (marriage announcement)

Therefore a man leaves his father and his mother and cleaves to his wife, and they become one flesh. (Gen. 2:24, Mark 10:7–9)

For this reason a man shall leave his father and mother and be joined to his wife, and the two shall become one flesh. So they are no longer two but one flesh. What therefore God has joined together, let not man put asunder. (Mark 10:7–9)

Apple of the eye, he kept him as the apple of his eye. (Deut. 32:10, Ps. 17:8, Prov. 7:2)

Bad company ruins good morals. (1 Cor. 15:33)

Evil for Evil. Do not return evil for evil or reviling for reviling. (1 Pet. 3:9)

Eye for Eye. If any harm follows, then you shall give life for life, eye for eye, tooth for tooth, hand for hand, foot for foot, burn for burn, wound for wound, stripe for stripe. (Exod. 21:23–25)

You have heard that is was said, "an eye for an eye and a tooth for a tooth." But I say to you, do not resist one who is evil. But if any one strikes you on the right cheek, turn to him the other also; and if any one would sue you and take your coat, let him have your cloak as well. (Matt. 5:38)

Forgive and you shall be forgiven. For if you forgive men their trespasses, your heavenly Father also will forgive you. (Matt. 6:14–15)

For the love of money is the root of all evils. (1 Tim. 6:10, Matt. 6:24)

Galeed. The Lord watch between you and me, when we are absent one from the other. (covenant between Laban and Jacob, God was their witness) this saying is often inscribed on jewelry. (Gen. 31:49)

Hairs of your head are numbered. Why, even the hairs of your head are all numbered. (Luke 12:7)

Judge not that you be not judged. (Matt. 7:1)

Let your Yes be Yes, and No be No. Let what you say be simply "Yes" or "No"; anything more than this comes from evil. (Matt. 5:37)

Love your neighbor as yourself. But you shall love your neighbor as yourself: I am the Lord. (Lev. 19:18, Gal. 5:14)

To obey is better than sacrifice. (1 Sam. 15:22)

O Ye of little faith. "O man of little faith, why did you doubt?" (Matt. 14:31)

Pink skies in the morning, sailor's warning, pink at night, sailor's delight. When it is evening, you say, "It will be fair weather; for the sky is red. And in the morning, "It will be stormy today, for the sky is red and threatening." (Matt. 16:2–3)

Spare the rod and spoil the child. He who spares the rod hates his son, but he who loves him is diligent to discipline him. (Prov. 13:24)

Vengeance is mine, I will repay. (Rom. 12:19, Heb. 10:30)

Where your treasure is so will your heart be. For where your treasure is, there will your heart be also. (Matt. 6:21)

Power

But for this purpose have I let you live, to show you My **power,** so that My name may be declared throughout all the earth. (Exod. 9:16)

Thy right hand, O Lord, glorious in **power**, Thy right hand, O Lord, shatters the enemy. (Exod. 15:6)

And now, I pray Thee, let Thy **power** of the Lord be great as Thou has promised. (Num. 14:17)

You shall remember the Lord your God, for it is He who gives you **power** to get wealth. (Deut. 8:18)

Every place on which the sole of your foot treads shall be yours; your territory shall be from the wilderness and Lebanon and from the River, the river Euphrates, to the western sea. No man shall be able to stand against you; the Lord our God will lay the fear of you and the dread of you upon all the land that you shall tread. (Deut. 11:24, 25)

Yea, by Thee I can crush a troop, and by my God I can leap over a wall. He trains my hands for war, so that my arms can bend a bow of bronze. For Thou didst gird me with **strength** for the battle. (2 Sam. 22:30, 35, 40)

Terrible is God in His sanctuary, the God of Israel, He gives **power** and strength to His people. (Ps. 68:35)

I will be give you the keys of the kingdom of heaven, and whatever you bind on earth shall be bound in heaven, and whatever you loose on earth shall be loosed in heaven. (Matt. 16:19)

All **authority** in heaven and on earth has been given to Me. (Matt. 28:18)

And Jesus returned in the **power** of the Spirit into Galilee. (Luke 4:14)

Behold, I have given you **authority** to tread upon serpents and scorpions, and over all the **power** of the enemy; and nothing shall hurt you. (Luke 10:19)

But to all who received Him, who believed in His name, He gave **power**. (John 1:12)

But you shall receive **power** when the Holy Spirit has come upon you. (Acts 1:8)

And what is the immeasurable greatness of His **power** in us who believe. (Eph. 1:19)

Now to Him who by the **power** at work within us is able to do far more abundantly than all that we ask or think. (Eph. 3:20)

May you be strengthened with all **power**, according to His glorious might. (Col. 1:11)

For God did not give us a spirit of timidity but a spirit of **power** and love and self-control. (2 Tim. 1:7)

By faith Sarah herself received **power** to conceive, even when she was past the age, since she considered Him faithful who had promised. (Heb. 11:11)

He who conquers and who keeps My works until the end, I will give him **power** over the nations. (Rev. 2:26)

Saying with a loud voice, "Worthy is the Lamb who was slain to receive **power** and wealth and wisdom and might and honor and glory and blessing! (Rev. 5:12)

Prayer

Yet have regard to the **prayer** of Thy servant and to his supplication, O Lord my God, hearkening to the cry and to the **prayer** which Thy servant prays before Thee this day. (1 Kings 8:28)

Let Thy eyes be open to the **supplication** of Thy servant, and to the **supplication** of Thy people Israel, giving ear to them whenever they call to Thee. (1 Kings 8:52)

If my people who are called by my name humble themselves, and **pray** and seek my face, and turn from their wicked ways, then I will hear from heaven, and will forgive their sin and heal their land. (2 Chron. 7:14)

Be gracious to me, and hear my **prayer**. (Ps. 4:1)

Give ear to my words, O Lord; give heed to my groaning. Hearken to the sound of my cry, my King and my God, for to Thee do I **pray**. (Ps. 5:1–2)

Evening and morning and at noon I utter my complaint and moan, and He will hear my voice. (Ps. 55:17)

The Lord is far from the wicked, but He hears the **prayer** of the righteous. (Prov. 15:29)

If one turns away his ear from hearing the law, even his **prayer** is an abomination. (Prov. 28:9)

Therefore I tell you whatever you ask in **prayer**, believe that you have received it, and it will be yours. (Mark 11:24)

And he told them a parable, to the effect that they ought always to **pray** and not lose heart. (Luke 18:1)

Rejoice in your hope, be patient in tribulation, be constant in **prayer**. (Rom. 12:12)

Pray at all times in the Spirit, with all **prayer** and supplication. (Eph. 6:18)

But in everything by **prayer** and supplication with thanksgiving let your request be made known to God. (Phil. 4:6)

Pray constantly. (1 Thess. 5:17)

In the days of His flesh, Jesus offered up **prayers** and supplications, with loud cries and tears, to Him who was able to save Him from death. (Heb. 5:7)

Is any among you suffering? Let him **pray**. And the **prayer** of faith will save the sick man, and the Lord will raise him up; **pray** for one another, that you may be healed. The **prayer** of a righteous man has great power in its effects. (James 5:13, 15, 16)

For the eyes of the Lord are upon the righteous, and His ears are open to their **prayer**. (1 Pet. 3:12)

Protection

Behold, I send an angel before you, to **guard you** on the way and to bring you to the place which I have prepared. (Exod. 23:20)

Do not be afraid or dismayed; be strong and of good courage; for thus the Lord will do to all your enemies against whom you fight. (Josh. 10:25)

And that all this assembly may know that the Lord saves not with sword and spear; for the battle is the Lord's and He will give you into our hand. (1 Sam. 17:47)

He reached from on high, He took me, He drew me out of many waters. He delivered me from my strong enemy, from those who hated me; for they were too mighty for me. They came upon me in the day of my calamity; but the Lord was my stay. He brought me forth into a broad place; He delivered me, because He delighted in me. (2 Sam. 22:17–20)

The promise of the Lord proves true; He is a **shield** for all those who take refuge in Him. This God is my strong refuge, and has made my way safe. (2 Sam. 22:31, 33)

In the covert of Thy presence Thou **hidest** them from the plots of men; Thou **holdest** them safe under Thy **shelter** from the strife of tongues. (Ps. 31:20)

The angel of the Lord **encamps around** those who fear Him, and delivers them. (Ps. 34:7)

For He will give His angels charge of you to **guard** you in all your ways. (Ps. 91:11)

He delivers them for the hand of the wicked. (Ps. 97:10)

The Lord will **keep** your going out and your coming in from this time forth and for evermore. (Ps. 121:8)

But he who listens to Me will dwell **secure** and will be at ease, without dread of evil. (Prov. 1:33)

He is a **shield** to those who walk in integrity. (Prov. 2:8)

He is a **shield** to those who take refuge in Him. (Prov. 30:5)

My people will abide in a peaceful habitation, in **secure dwellings**, and in quiet resting places. (Isa. 32:18)

Finally, be strong in the Lord and in the strength of His might. Put on the **whole armor of God** that you may be able to stand against the wiles of the devil. For we are not contending against flesh and blood, but against the principalities against the powers, against the world rulers of this present darkness, against the spiritual hosts of wickedness in the heavenly places. Therefore take the whole armor of God, that you may be able to withstand in the evil day, and having done all, to stand. Stand therefore having **girded your loins with truth**, and having **put on the breastplate of righteousness**, and **having shod your feet with the equipment of the gospel of peace**, besides all these, **taking the shield of faith**, with which you can quench all the flaming darts of the evil one. And **take the helmet of salvation**, and **the sword of the Spirit**, which is the word of God. (Eph. 6:10–17)

Provisions

And God said, Behold, I have given you every **plant** yielding seed which is upon the face of all the earth, and every **tree** with seed in its fruit; you shall have them for food. (Gen. 1:29)

As it is said to this day, "On the mount of the Lord it shall be **provided**." (Gen. 22:14)

For I will cast out nations before you, and enlarge your **borders**. (Exod. 34:24)

He has filled them with **ability** to do every sort of work done by a craftsman or by a designer or by an embroiderer. (Exod. 35:35)

But I have said to you, you shall inherit their **land**, and I will give it to you to possess, a land flowing with milk and honey. (Lev. 20:24)

If you walk in My statutes and observe My commandments and do them, then I will give you your **rains** in their season, and the land shall yield its **increase**, and the trees of the field shall yield their **fruit**. And your threshing shall last to the time of **vintage**, and the vintage shall last to the time for sowing; and you shall eat your **bread** to the full, and dwell in your land securely. And I will give **peace** in the land, and you shall lie down, and none shall make you afraid; and I will remove evil beasts from the land, and the sword shall not go through your land. And you shall chase your enemies, and they shall fall before you by the sword. (Lev. 26:3–7)

Is the Lord's hand shortened? (Num. 11:23)

The Lord your God who goes before you will Himself fight for you. (Deut. 1:30)

You shall not fear them; for it is the Lord your God who fights for you. (Deut. 3:22)

And He will give their kings into your hand, and you shall make their name perish from under heaven; not a man shall be able to stand against you. (Deut. 7:24)

That He might make you know that man does not live by bread alone, but that man lives by every thing that proceeds out of the mouth of the Lord. (Deut. 8:3)

Know therefore this day that He who goes over before you as a devouring fire is the Lord your God; He will destroy them and subdue them before you. (Deut. 9:3)

He will give the **rain** for your land in its season, the early rain and the later rain, that you may gather in your **grain** and your **wine** and your **oil**. And He will give **grass** in your fields for your cattle, and you shall eat and be full. (Deut. 11:14)

Every place on which the sole of your foot treads shall be yours; No man shall be able to stand against you; the Lord your God will lay the fear of you and the dread of you upon all the land that you shall tread. (Deut. 11:24, 25)

The Lord will cause your enemies who rise against you to be defeated before you; The Lord will command the **blessing** upon you in your **barns,** and in all that you undertake; and He will bless you in the land which the Lord your God gives you. The Lord will **establish you** as a people holy to himself. (Deut. 28:7–9)

Every place that the sole of your foot will tread upon I have given to you. (Josh. 1:3)

For it is the Lord your God who has fought for you. (Josh. 23:3)

The Lord is with you, you mighty man of valor. (Judg. 6:12)

He raises up the poor from the dust; and lifts the needy from the ash heap. (1 Sam. 2:8)

Now therefore stand still and see this great thing, which the Lord will do before your eyes. (1 Sam. 12:16)

For He has made with me an everlasting **covenant**, ordered in all things and secure. (2 Sam. 23:5)

And God is able to **provide** you with every blessing in abundance, so that you may always have enough of everything and may **provide** in abundance for every good work. He who **supplies seed** to the sower and **bread** for food will supply and multiply your resources. (2 Cor. 9:8, 10)

And my God will supply **every need** of yours according to His riches in glory in Christ Jesus. (Phil. 4:19)

As for the rich in this world, charge them not to be haughty, nor to set their hopes on uncertain riches but on God who richly **furnishes** us with everything to enjoy. (1 Tim. 6:17)

Rainbows

I set My **bow** in the cloud, and it shall be a sign of the covenant between Me and the earth. When I bring clouds over the earth and the **bow** is seen in the clouds, I will remember My covenant which is between Me and you. (Gen. 9:13)

Like the appearance of the **bow** that is in the cloud on the day of rain, so was the appearance of the brightness round about. (Ezek. 1:28)

And round the throne was a **rainbow** that looked like an emerald. (Rev. 4:3)

Then I saw another mighty angel coming down from heaven, wrapped in a cloud, with a **rainbow** over his head, and his face was like the sun. (Rev. 10:1)

Renewal of Mind

A **tranquil mind** gives life to the flesh. (Prov. 14:30)

And you will know the truth, and the **truth** will make you free. (John 8:32)

Do not be conformed to this world but be transformed by the **renewa**l of your **mind**. (Rom. 12:2)

And be **renewed** in the spirit of **your minds**, and put on the new nature, created after the likeness of God in true righteousness and holiness. (Eph. 4:23)

Have this mind among yourselves, which is yours in Christ Jesus. (Phil. 2:5)

So shun youthful passions and aim at righteousness, faith, love, and peace, along with those who call upon the Lord from a pure heart. (2 Tim. 2:22)

Therefore **gird up** your **minds**, be sober, set your hope fully upon the grace that is coming to you at the revelation of Jesus Christ. (1 Pet. 1:13)

Finally, all of you, have unity of spirit, sympathy, love of the brethren, a tender heart and a **humble mind**. Always be prepared to make a defense to any one who calls you to account for the hope that is in you, yet do it with gentleness and reverence. (1 Pet. 8, 15)

Repentance

And also the Glory of Israel will not lie or **repent**; for He is not a man, that He should **repent**. (1 Sam. 15:29)

And when the angel stretched forth His hand toward Jerusalem to destroy it, the Lord **repented** of the evil, It is enough; now stay your hand. (2 Sam. 24:16)

I acknowledged my sin to Thee, and I did not hide my iniquity; I said, I will **confess** my transgressions to the Lord; then Thou didst forgive the guilt of my sin. (Ps. 32:5)

John the baptizer appeared in the wilderness preaching a baptism of **repentance** for the forgiveness of sins. (Mark 1:4)

And he went into all the region about the Jordan, preaching a baptism of **repentance** for the forgiveness of sins. (Luke 3:3)

But unless you **repent** you will all likewise perish. (Luke 13:5)

For godly grief produces a **repentance** that leads to salvation and brings no regret. (2 Cor. 7:10)

Rest

And He **rested** on the seventh day from all His work which He had done. (Gen. 2:2)

Six days you shall do your work, but on the seventh day you shall **rest**. (Exod. 23:12)

I lie down and **sleep**; I wake again, for the Lord sustains me. (Ps. 3:5)

When you lie down, your **sleep** will be sweet. (Prov. 3:24)

Blessed be the Lord who has given **rest** to His people Israel, according to all that He promised. (1 Kings 8:56)

Come to Me, all who labor and are heavy laden, and I will give you **rest**. (Matt. 11:28)

Come away by yourselves to a lonely place, and **rest** for a while. (Mark 6:31)

So then, there remains a Sabbath **rest** for the people of God; for whoever enters God's **rest** also ceases from his labors as God did from His. (Heb. 4:9)

That they may **rest** from their labors, for their deeds follow them! (Rev. 14:13)

Resurrection

For in the **resurrection** they neither marry nor are given in marriage, but are like angels in heaven. (Matt. 22:30)

In a moment, in the twinkling of an eye, at the last trumpet. For the trumpet will sound, and the dead will be raised imperishable, and we shall be changed. For this perishable nature must put on the imperishable, and this mortal nature must put on immortality. (1 Cor. 15:52–53)

I tell you, many will come from the east and west and sit at the table with Abraham, Isaac, and Jacob in the kingdom of heaven. (Matt. 8:11)

For if we have been united with Him in a death like His, we shall certainly be united with Him in a **resurrection** like His. (Rom. 6:5)

Blessed, be the God and Father of our Lord Jesus Christ. By His great mercy we have been born anew to a living hope through the **resurrection** of Jesus Christ from the dead, and to an inheritance which is imperishable, undefiled, and unfading, kept in heaven for you, who by God's power are guarded through faith for a salvation ready to be revealed in the last time. (1 Pet. 1:3–5)

And come forth, those who have done good, to the **resurrection** of life, and those who have done evil, to the **resurrection** of judgement. (John 5:29)

Righteousness

So you shall keep the commandments of the Lord your God, by walking in His ways and by fearing Him. (Deut. 8:6)

The Lord rewards every man for his **righteousness** and his faithfulness. (1 Sam. 26:23)

The Lord rewarded me according to my **righteousness**; according to the cleanness of my hands He recompensed me. (2 Sam. 22:21)

Then hear thou in heaven, and act, and judge Thy servants, condemning the guilty by bringing his conduct upon his own head, and vindicating the righteous by rewarding him according to his **righteousness**. (1 Kings 8:32)

For the Lord is **righteous**, He loves **righteous** deeds; the upright shall behold His face. (Ps. 11:7)

He leads me in paths of **righteousness** for His name's sake. (Ps. 23:3)

Who shall ascend the hill of the Lord? And who shall stand in His holy place? He who has clean hands and a **pure heart**, who does not lift up his soul to what is false, and does not swear deceitfully. He will receive blessing from the Lord, and vindication from the God of his salvation. (Ps. 24:3–5)

I have been young, and now am old; yet I have not seen the **righteous** forsaken or his children begging bread. (Ps. 37:25)

No good thing does the Lord withhold from those who walk **uprightly**. (Ps. 84:11)

The mouth of the **righteous** is a fountain of life. (Prov. 10:11)

But the desire of the **righteous** will be granted. (Prov. 10:24)

Sow for yourselves, **righteousness,** reap the fruit of steadfast love. (Hosea 10:12)

Blessed are those who hunger and thirst for **righteousness,** for they shall be satisfied. (Matt. 5:6)

But seek first His kingdom and His **righteousness,** and all these things shall be yours as well. (Matt. 6:33)

But now the **righteousness** of God has been manifested apart from law, the righteousness of God through faith in Jesus Christ for all who believe. (Rom. 3:21–22)

For the kingdom of God is not food and drink but **righteousness** and peace and joy in the Holy Spirit. (Rom. 14:17)

Thus Abraham "believed God, and it was reckoned to him as **righteousness**." (Gal. 3:6)

Not having a **righteousness** of my own, based on law, but that which is through faith in Christ, the righteousness from God that depends on faith. (Phil. 3:9)

For the moment all discipline seems painful rather than pleasant; later it yields the peaceful fruit of **righteousness** to those who have been trained by it. (Heb. 12:11)

Sabbath

This is what the Lord has commanded: Tomorrow is a day of solemn rest, a holy **Sabbath** to the Lord; for today is a Sabbath to the Lord. So the people rested on the seventh day. (Exod. 16:23, 25, 30)

You shall keep My **Sabbaths** and reverence My sanctuary: I am the Lord. (Lev. 19:30)

Six days shall work be done; but on the seventh day is a **Sabbath** of solemn rest, a holy convocation; you shall do no work. (Lev. 23:3)

You shall keep My **Sabbaths** and reverence My sanctuary: I am the Lord. (Lev. 26:2)

Observe the **Sabbath** day, to keep it holy, as the Lord your God commanded you. Six days you shall labor and do all your work; but the seventh day is a **Sabbath** to the Lord your God. (Deut. 5:12–14)

Salvation

Fear not, stand firm, and see the **salvation** of the Lord. (Exod. 14:13)

The Lord is my strength and my song, and He has become my **salvation**. (Exod. 15:2)

The Lord lives; and blessed be my rock, and exalted be my God, the rock of my **salvation**. (2 Sam. 22:47)

Unless one is **born anew**, he cannot see the kingdom of God. (John 3:3)

For God sent the Son into the world, not to condemn the world, but that the world might be **saved** through Him. (John 3:17)

No one can come to me unless the Father who sent Me draws Him; and I will raise him up at the last day. Truly, truly, I say to you, He who believes has **eternal life**. (John 6:44, 47)

I am the way, and the truth, and the life; no one comes to the Father, but by Me. (John 14:6)

And there is **salvation** in no one else, for there is no other name under heaven given among men by which we must be saved. (Acts 4:12)

Believe in the Lord Jesus, and you will be **saved,** you and your household. (Acts 16:31)

For I am not ashamed of the gospel: it is the power of God for **salvation** to every one who has faith, to the Jew first and also to the Greek. (Rom. 1:16)

If you confess with your lips that Jesus is Lord and believe in your heart that God raised Him from the dead, you will be **saved**. For man believes with his heart and so is justified, and he confesses with his lips and so is **saved**. The scripture says, No one who believes in Him will be put to shame. For there is no distinction between Jew and Greek; the same Lord is Lord of all and bestows His riches upon all who call upon Him. For everyone who calls upon the name of the Lord will be **saved**. (Rom. 10:9–13)

For by grace you have been **saved** through faith. (Eph. 2:8)

For God has not destined us for wrath, but to obtain **salvation** through our Lord Jesus Christ. (1 Thess. 5:9)

Because God chose you from the beginning to be **saved,** through sanctification by the spirit. (2 Thess. 2:13)

For the grace of God has appeared for the **salvation** of all men. (Titus 2:11)

For it was fitting that He, for whom and by whom all things exist, in bringing many sons to glory, should make the pioneer of their **salvation** perfect through suffering. (Heb. 2:10)

And being made perfect He became the source of eternal **salvation** to all who obey Him. (Heb. 5:9)

Consequently He is able for all time to **save** those who draw near to God through Him. (Heb. 7:25)

As the outcome of your faith you obtain the **salvation** of your souls. (1 Pet. 1:9)

And count the forbearance of our Lord as **salvation**. (2 Pet. 3:15)

After this I heard what seemed to be the loud voice of a great multitude in heaven, crying, Hallelujah! **Salvation** and glory and power belong to our God. (Rev. 19:1)

Sanctification

And the Lord said to Moses, Say to the people of Israel, You shall keep my Sabbaths, for this is a sign between Me and you throughout your generations, that you may know that I, the Lord, **sanctify** you. (Exod. 31:12)

You shall consecrate Him, for He offers the bread of your God; He shall be holy to you; for I the Lord, who **sanctify** you, am holy. (Lev. 21:8)

And you shall not profane My holy name, but I will be hallowed among the people of Israel; I am the Lord who **sanctify** you. (Lev. 22:32)

Husbands, love your wives, as Christ loved the church and gave Himself up for her, that He might **sanctify** her, having cleansed her by the washing of water with the word. (Eph. 5:25–26)

And by that will we have been **sanctified** though the offering of the body of Jesus Christ once for all. (Heb. 10:10)

So Jesus also suffered outside the gate in order to **sanctify** the people through His own blood. (Heb. 13:12)

Seasons/Times

And God said, let there be lights in the firmament of the heavens to separate the day from the night; and let them be for signs and for **seasons** and for days and years. (Gen. 1:14)

While the earth remains, **seedtime** and **harvest**, **cold and heat**, **summer** and **winter**, day and night, shall not cease. (Gen. 8:22)

For everything there is a **season**, and **a time** for every matter under heaven: a **time** to be born, and a **time** to die; a **time** to plant, and a **time** to pluck up what is planted; a **time** to kill, and a **time** to heal; a **time** to break down, and a **time** to build up; a **time** to weep, and a **time** to laugh; a **time** to mourn, and a **time** to dance; a **time** to cast away stones, and a **time** to gather stones together; a **time** to embrace, and a **time** to refrain from embracing; a **time** to seek, and a **time** to lose; a **time** to keep, and a **time** to cast away; a **time** to rend, and a **time** to sew; a **time** to keep silence, and a **time** to speak; a **time** to love and a **time** to hate; a **time** for war, and a **time** for peace. (Eccles. 3:1–8)

He has made everything beautiful in its **time**. (Eccles. 3:11)

Thou hast fixed all the bounds of the earth; thou hast made **summer** and **winter**. (Ps. 74:17)

Thou hast made the moon to mark the **seasons**; the sun knows its time for setting. (Ps. 104:19)

He changes **times** and **seasons**. (Dan. 2:21)

But as to the **times** and the **seasons**, brethren, you have no need to have anything written to you. For you yourselves know well that the day of the Lord will come like a thief in the night. (1 Thess. 5:1)

But do not ignore this one fact, beloved, that with the Lord one day is as a thousand years, and a thousand years as one day. (2 Pet. 3:8)

Length of Days / Long Life

Then the Lord said, my spirit shall not abide in man for ever, for He is flesh, but his days shall be a **hundred and twenty years**. (Gen. 6:3)

I will fulfil the **number** of your days. (Exod. 23:26)

And if you will walk in my ways, keeping my statutes and my commandments, as your father David walked, then I will **lengthen your days**. (1 Kings 3:14)

And if the Lord had not shortened the days, no human being would be saved; but for the sake of the elect, whom He chose, He **shortened the days**. (Mark 13:20)

Self-Control

I will **guard** my ways, that I may not sin with my tongue; I will bridle my mouth. (Ps. 39:1)

He who is slow to anger is better than the mighty, and he who **rules his spirit** than he who takes a city. (Prov. 16:32)

A fool gives full vent to this anger, but a wise man **quietly holds it back**. (Prov. 29:11)

We will drink no wine. (Jer. 35:6)

For we all make many mistakes, and if any one makes no mistakes in what he says he is a perfect man, able to **bridle** the whole body also. (James 3:2)

For this very reason make every effort to supplement your faith with virtue, and virtue with knowledge, and knowledge with **self-control**. (2 Pet. 1:5)

Sins

Adultery

If a man commits **adultery** with the wife of his neighbor, both the adulterer and the adulteress shall be put to death. (Lev. 20:10)

Of Flesh

If a man lies with a male as with a woman, both of them have committed an **abomination**; they shall be put to death, If a man lies with a beast, he shall be put to death. (Lev. 20:13, 15)

If a woman approaches any beast and lies with it, you shall kill the woman and the beast; If a man takes his sister and sees her nakedness, and she sees his nakedness, it is a shameful thing, and they shall be cut off in the sight of the children of their people; If a man lies with a woman having her sickness, and uncovers her nakedness, and she has uncovered the fountain of her blood; both of them shall be cut off from among their people. You shall not uncover the nakedness of your mother's sister or of your father's sister, they shall bear their **iniquity**. If a man lies with his uncle's wife, they shall bear their **sin,** they shall die childless. If a man takes his brother's wife, it is impurity; he has uncovered his brother's nakedness, they shall be childless. (Lev. 20:16–21)

General

If you do well, will you not be accepted? And if you do not do well, **sin** is couching at the door; its desire is for you, but you must master it. (Gen. 4:7)

Do not fear; for God has come to prove you, and that the fear of Him may be before your eyes, that you may not **sin**. (Exod. 20:20)

Nevertheless, in the day when I visit, I will visit their **sin** upon them. (Exod. 32:34)

And say to the people of Israel, whoever curses his God shall bear his **sin**. (Lev. 24:15)

But if you will not do so, behold, you have **sinned** against the Lord; and be sure your **sin** will find you out. (Num. 32:23)

Every man shall be put to death for his own **sin**. (Deut. 24:16)

I have laid up Thy word in my heart, that I might not **sin** against Thee. (Ps. 119:11)

The soul that **sins** shall die. (Ezek. 18:20)

Truly, I say to you, all **sins** will be forgiven the sons of men, and whatever blasphemies they utter; but whoever blasphemes against the Holy Spirit never has forgiveness, but is guilty of an eternal **sin**. (Mark 3:28–30)

For I will be merciful toward their iniquities, and I will remember their **sins** no more. (Heb. 8:12)

He has appeared once for all at the end of the age to put away **sin** by the sacrifice of Himself. (Heb. 9:26)

But in these sacrifices there is a reminder of **sin** year after year. For it is impossible that the blood of bulls and goats should take away **sins**. In burnt offerings and **sin** offerings thou hast taken no pleasure. (Heb. 10:3–4, 6)

For if we **sin** deliberately after receiving the knowledge of the truth, there no longer remains a sacrifice for **sins**, but a fearful prospect of judgment. (Heb. 10:26, 27)

Therefore, since we are surrounded by so great a cloud of witnesses, let us also lay aside every weight, and **sin** which clings so closely, and let us run with perseverance the race that is set before us. (Heb. 12:1)

But if you show partiality, you commit **sin**. (James 2:9)

Whoever knows what is right to do and fails to do it, for him it is **sin**. (James 4:17)

But if we walk in the light, as He is in the light, we have fellowship with one another, and the blood of Jesus His Son cleanses us from all **sin**. If we confess our **sins**, He is faithful and just, and will forgive our **sins** and cleanse us from all unrighteousness. (1 John 1:7, 9)

I am writing to you, little children, because your **sins** are forgiven for His sake. (1 John 2:12)

Every one who commits **sin** is guilty of lawlessness; **sin** is lawlessness. You know that He appeared to take away **sins**, and in Him there is no **sin**. No one who abides in Him **sins**; no one who **sins** has either seen Him or known Him. He who commits **sin is** of the devil; for the devil has **sinned** from the beginning. No one born of God commits **sin**. (1 John 3:4–9)

If anyone sees his brother committing what is not a mortal **sin**, he will ask, and God will give him life for those whose **sin** is not mortal. There is **sin** which is mortal; I do not say that one is to pray for that. All wrongdoing is **sin,** but there is **sin** which is not mortal. (1 John 5:16–17)

To Him who loves us and has freed us from our **sins** by His blood. (Rev. 1:5)

Speaking (Positive)

And you shall **speak** to him and put the words in his mouth; and I will be with your mouth and with his mouth, and will teach you what you shall do. (Exod. 4:15)

You shall not utter a false report. You shall not join hands with a wicked man, to be a malicious witness. (Exod. 23:1)

And you shall **not swear** by My name falsely, and so profane the name of your God. You shall not curse the deaf or put a stumbling block before the blind. (Lev. 19:2–4, 11–12)

For every one who **curses** his father or his mother shall be put to death. (Lev. 20:9)

When you make a vow to the Lord your God, you shall not be slack to pay it; for the Lord your God will surely require it of you, and it would be sin in you. But if you refrain from vowing, it shall be no sin in you. You shall **be careful** to perform **what has passed your lips**, for you have voluntarily vowed to the Lord your God what you have promised with your mouth. (Deut. 23:21–23)

If you are **snared** in the **utterance of your lips**, caught in the words of our mouth; then do this, my son, and save yourself, for you have come into your neighbor's power; go, hasten, and importune your neighbor. (Prov. 6:2–3)

The words of a man's mouth are deep waters. (Prov. 18:4)

Death and life are in the power of the tongue, and those who love it will eat its fruits. (Prov. 18:21)

Be not rash with your mouth, nor let your heart be hasty to utter a word before God, for God is in heaven, and you upon earth; therefore, let your words be few. (Eccles. 5:2)

For by your words you will be justified, and by your words you will be condemned. (Matt. 12:37)

God chose what is low and despised in the world, even things that are not, to bring to nothing things that are, so that no human being might boast in the presence of God. therefore, as it is written, "Let him who boasts, boast of the Lord." (1 Cor. 1:28, 29, 31)

Let **no evil talk** come out of your mouths, but only such as is good for edifying, as fits the occasion, that it may **impart grace** to those who hear. Let all bitterness and wrath and anger and clamor and **slander** be put away from you, with all malice, and be kind to one another. (Eph. 4:29–31)

But now put them all away: anger, wrath, malice, **slande**r, and **foul talk** from your mouth. (Col. 3:8)

Let your speech always be **gracious**, seasoned with salt, so that you may know how you ought to answer every one. (Col. 4:6)

But just as we have been approved by God to be entrusted with the gospel, so we speak, not to please men, but to please God who tests our hearts. (1 Thess. 2:4)

Therefore encourage one another and build one another up. (1 Thess. 5:11)

Avoid such **godless chatter**, for it will lead people into more and more ungodliness, and their talk will eat its way like gangrene. (2 Tim. 2:16–17)

But avoid stupid controversies, genealogies, **dissensions**, and **quarrels** over the law, for they are unprofitable and futile. (Titus 3:9)

Do not **speak evil** against one another, brethren. (James 4:11)

But above all, my brethren, do not swear, either by heaven or by earth or with any other oath but let your yes be yes and your no be no, that you may not fall under condemnation. (James 5:12)

Let him keep his tongue from **evil** and his lips from **speaking guile**. (1 Pet. 3:10)

Standing (Ground)

The Lord will fight for you, and you have only to **be still**. (Exod. 14:14)

For freedom Christ has set us free; **stand fast** therefore, and do not submit again to a yoke of slavery. (Gal. 5:1)

Put on the whole armor of God, that you may be able **to stand** against the wiles of the devil. (Eph. 6:11)

Therefore take the whole armor of God that you may be able to withstand in the evil day, and having done all **to stand**. **Stand** therefore, having girded your loins with truth and having put on the breastplate of righteousness. (Eph. 6:13–14)

So then, brethren, **stand firm** and hold to the traditions which you were taught by us, either by word of mouth or by letter. (2 Thess. 2:15)

Submit yourselves therefore to God. Resist the devil and he will flee from you. (James 4:7)

I have written briefly to you, exhorting and declaring that this is the true grace of God; **stand fast** in it. (1 Pet. 5:12)

Strength

The Lord is my **strength** and my song. (Exod. 15:2)

Thou hast guided them by Thy **strength** to Thy holy abode. (Exod. 15:13)

Be **strong** and of good courage, do not fear or be in dread of them; Be **strong** and of good courage. (Deut. 31:6, 23)

Your bars shall be iron and bronze; and as your days, so shall your **strength** be. (Deut. 33:25)

Be **strong** and of good courage; Be **strong** and of good courage; be not frightened, neither be dismayed. (Josh. 1, 6, 9)

Do not be afraid or dismayed; be **strong** and of good courage. (Josh. 10:25)

For as the man is, so is his **strength**. (Judg. 8:21)

David **strengthened** himself in the Lord his God. (1 Sam. 30:6)

Yea, by Thee I can crush a troop, and by my God I can leap over a wall. (2 Sam. 22:30)

For thou didst gird me with **strength** for the battle. (2 Sam. 22:40)

Be **strong** and of good courage, and do it. Fear not, be not dismayed; for the Lord God, even my God, is with you. (1 Chron. 28:20)

For the joy of the Lord is your **strength**. (Neh. 8:10)

Wait for the Lord; be **strong**, and let your heart take courage. (Ps. 27:14)

The Lord is my **strength** and my shield; in Him my heart trusts. (Ps. 28:7)

May the Lord give **strength** to His people! (Ps. 29:11)

God is our refuge and **strength**, a very present help in trouble. (Ps. 46:1)

Summon Thy might, O God; show Thy **strength,** O God, Thou who has wrought for us. (Ps. 68:28)

The Lord is my **strength** and my song; He has become my salvation. (Ps. 118:14)

On the day I called, Thou didst answer me, my **strength** of soul Thou didst increase. (Ps. 138:3)

If you faint in the day of adversity, your **strength** is small. (Prov. 24:10)

In returning and rest you shall be saved; in quietness and in trust shall be your **strength**. (Isa. 30:15)

He gives power to the faint, and to him who has no might He increases **strength**. (Isa. 40:29)

But they who wait for the Lord shall renew their **strength**, they shall mount up with wings like eagles, they shall run and not be weary, they shall walk and not faint. (Isa. 40:31)

Fear not, for I am with you, be not dismayed, for I am your God; I will **strengthen** you, I will help you, I will uphold you with my victorious right hand. (Isa. 41:10)

Be **strong** in the Lord and in the **strength** of His might. (Eph. 6:10)

I can do all things in Him who **strengthens** me. (Phil. 4:13)

But the Lord is faithful; He will **strengthen** you and guard you from evil. (2 Thess. 3:3)

The God of all grace, who has called you to His eternal glory in Christ, will Himself restore, establish, and **strengthen** you. (1 Pet. 5:10)

Suffering for Christ / Afflictions / Trials

Take heed lest you forget the Lord your God, then your heart be lifted up, and you forget the Lord your God, who brought you out of the land of Egypt, out of the house of bondage, who led you through the great and terrible wilderness, with its fiery serpents and scorpions and thirsty ground where there was no water, who brought you water out of the flinty rock, who fed you in the wilderness with manna which your fathers did not know, that He might humble you and test you, to do you good in the end. (Deut. 8:11, 14, 16)

I want you to know, brethren, that what has happened to me has really served to advance the gospel. (Phil. 1:12)

For His sake I have **suffered** the loss of all things, and count them as refuse, in order that I may gain Christ, and be found in Him, not having a righteousness of my own, based on law, but that which is through faith in Christ, the righteousness from God that depends on faith; that I may know Him and the power of His resurrection, and may share His **sufferings**, becoming like Him in His death. (Phil. 3:8–10)

Share in **suffering** as a good soldier of Christ Jesus. (2 Tim 2:3)

He considered abuse **suffered** for the Christ greater wealth than the treasure of Egypt, for he looked to the reward. By faith he left Egypt, not being afraid of the anger of the king; for he **endured** as seeing Him who is invisible. (Heb. 11:26, 27)

Count it all joy, my brethren, when you meet various **trials**, for you know that the **testing** of your faith produces steadfastness. And let steadfastness have its full effect, that you may be perfect and complete, lacking in nothing. (James 1:2–4)

In this you rejoice, though now for a little while you may have to **suffer** various trials, so that the genuineness of our faith, more precious than gold which though perishable is **tested** by fire, may redound to praise and glory and honor at the revelation of Jesus Christ. (1 Pet. 1:6–7)

For one is approved if, mindful of God, He **endures** pain while **suffering** unjustly. For what credit is it, if when you do wrong and are beaten for it you take it patiently? But if when you do right and **suffer** for it you take it patiently, you have God's approval. (1 Pet. 2:19–20)

But even if you do **suffer** for righteousness' sake, you will be blessed. For it is better to suffer for doing right, if that should be God's will, than for doing wrong. (1 Pet. 3:14, 17)

But rejoice in so far as you share Christ's **suffering,** that you may also rejoice and be glad when His glory is revealed. Yet if one **suffers** as a Christian, let him not be ashamed, but under that name let him glorify God. (1 Pet. 4:13, 16)

Therefore let those who **suffer** according to God's will do right and entrust their souls to a faithful Creator. (1 Pet. 4:19)

Resist him, firm in your faith, knowing that the same experience of **suffering** is required of your brotherhood throughout the world. And after you have **suffered** a little while, the God of all grace, who has called you to His eternal glory in Christ, will Himself restore, establish, and strengthen you. (1 Pet. 5:9–10)

Thanksgiving

Praise the Lord! O give **thanks** to the Lord, for He is good; for His steadfast love endures forever! (Ps. 106:1)

O give **thanks** to the Lord, for He is good; for His steadfast love endures forever! (Ps. 107:1)

But in everything by prayer and supplication with **thanksgiving** let your requests be made known to God. (Phil. 4:6)

Giving **thanks** to the Father, who has qualified us to share in the inheritance of the saints in light. (Col. 1:12)

As therefore you received Christ Jesus the Lord, so live in Him, rooted and built up in Him and established in the faith, just as you were taught, abounding in **thanksgiving**. (Col. 2:6–7)

Give **thanks** in all circumstances. (1 Thess. 5:18)

I **thank** my God always when I remember you in my prayers. (Phlm. 4)

Trust

O my God, in Thee I **trust**. (Ps. 25:2)

Trust in the Lord, and do good; so you will dwell in the land, and enjoy security. (Ps. 37:3)

Blessed is the man who makes the Lord his **trust**. (Ps. 40:4)

O Israel, **trust** in the Lord! He is their help and their shield. (Ps. 115:9)

For I **trust** in Thy word. (Ps. 119:42)

Trust in the Lord with all your heart, and do not rely on your own insight. (Prov. 3:5)

Behold, God is my salvation; I will **trust**, and will not be afraid. (Isa. 12:2)

Trust in the Lord forever, for the Lord God is an everlasting rock. (Isa. 26:4)

War Room Prayers: Nation

If my people who are called by my name humble themselves, and pray and seek My face, and turn from their wicked ways, then I will hear from heaven, and will forgive their sin and heal their land. (2 Chron. 7:14)

He trains my hands for **war**, so that my arms can bend a bow of bronze. (Ps. 18:34)

For Thou didst gird me with strength for the **battle**; Thou didst make my assailants sink under me. Thou didst make my enemies turn their backs to me, and those who hated me I destroyed. (Ps. 18:39–40)

Blessed is the nation whose God is the Lord, the people whom He has chosen as His heritage! (Ps. 33:12)

For Thou art my refuge, a strong tower against the enemy. (Ps. 61:3)

The fear of the Lord is the beginning of wisdom, and the knowledge of the Holy One is insight. (Prov. 9:10)

Righteousness exalts a nation, but sin is a reproach to any people. (Prov. 13:34)

In the year that King Uzziah died, I saw the Lord sitting upon a throne, high and lifted up; and His train filled the temple. (Isa. 6:1)

Arise, shine; for your light has come, and the glory of the Lord has risen upon you. (Isa. 60:1)

He changes times and seasons; He removes kings and sets up kings; He gives wisdom to the wise and knowledge to those who have understanding. (Dan. 2:21)

Thy kingdom come, Thy will be done, on earth as it is in heaven. (Matt. 6:10)

And I tell you, you are Peter, and on this rock I will build My church, and the powers of death shall not prevail against it. (Matt. 16:18)

Therefore come out from them, and be separate from them, says the Lord, and touch nothing unclean; then I will welcome you. (2 Cor. 6:17)

Blessed by the Lord, my rock, who **trains my hands for war**, and my **fingers for battle**. (Ps. 144:1)

Watchman

I also said to the people at that time, let every man and his servant pass the night within Jerusalem, that they may be a **guard** for us by night and may labor by day. (Neh. 4:22)

Upon your walls, O Jerusalem, I have set **watchmen;** all the day and all the night they shall never be silent. (Isa. 62:6)

And I sought for a man among them who should build up the wall and **stand in the breach** before me for the land, that I should not destroy it; but I found none. (Ezek. 22:30)

But take heed to yourselves lest your hearts be weighed down with dissipation and drunkenness and cares of this life, and that day come upon you suddenly like a snare; But **watch** at all times, praying that you may have strength to escape all these things that will take place. (Luke 21:34, 36)

Continue steadfastly in prayer, being **watchful** in it with thanksgiving. (Col. 4:2)

Be sober, be **watchful**. Your adversary the devil prowls around like a roaring lion, seeking some one to devour. (1 Pet. 5:8)

Weapons/Warfare

You are my hammer and **weapon of war**: with you I break nations in pieces; with you I destroy kingdoms. (Jer. 51:20)

Contend, O Lord, with those who contend with me; fight against those who fight against me! Take hold of shield and buckler, and rise for my help! Draw the spea and javelin against my pursuers! Say to my soul, "I am your deliverance." (Ps. 35:1–3)

For Thou art my refuge, a strong tower against the enemy. (Ps. 61:3)

With the Lord on my side I do not fear. What can man do to me? The Lord is on my side to help me; I shall look in triumph on those who hate me. All nations surrounded me; in the name of the Lord I cut them off! The Lord is my strength and my song. (Ps. 118:6, 7, 10, 14)

But when you pray, go into your room and shut the door and **pray** to your Father who is in secret; and your Father who sees in secret will reward you. (Matt. 6:6)

(*Spiritual warfare*) Pray then like this: "Our Father who art in heaven, Hallowed be Thy name. Thy kingdom come, Thy will be done, on earth as it is in heaven. Give us this day our daily bread; And forgive us our debts, as we also have forgiven our debtors; And lead us not into temptation, but deliver us from evil." (Matt. 6:9–13)

From the days of John the Baptist until now the kingdom of heaven has suffered violence, and men of violence take it by force. (Matt. 11:12)

I will give you the **keys of the kingdom** of heaven and whatever you bind on earth shall be bound in heaven, and whatever you loose on earth shall be loosed in heaven. (Matt. 16:19)

Truly, I say to you, whatever you bind on earth shall be bound in heaven, and whatever you loose on earth shall be loosed in heaven. Again, I say to you, if two of you agree on earth about anything they ask it will be done for them by My Father in heaven. For where two or three are gathered in My name, there am I in the midst of them. (Matt. 18:18–20)

But no one can enter a strong man's house and plunder his goods, unless he first binds the strong man; then indeed he may plunder his house. (Mark 3:27)

Behold, I have given you **authority** to tread upon serpents and scorpions, and over all the power of the enemy; and nothing shall hurt you. (Luke 10:19)

Seek His kingdom and these things shall be yours as well. (Luke 12:31)

Whatever you ask in My name, I will do it, that the Father may be gloried in the Son; if you ask anything in My name, I will do it. (John 14:13–14)

But God made us alive together with Christ and **raised us up** with Him and made us sit with Him in the heavenly places in Christ Jesus. (Eph. 2:4–6)

Finally, be strong in the Lord and in the strength of His might. Put on the **whole armor of God**, that you may be able to stand against the wiles of the devil. For we are not contending against flesh and blood, but against the principalities, against the powers, against the world rulers of this present darkness, against the spiritual host of wickedness in the heavenly places. Therefore, take the **whole armor of God,** that you may be able to withstand in the evil day, and having done all, to stand. Stand therefore, having **girded your loins with truth**, and having put on **the breastplate of righteousness**, and having shod your **feet** with the equipment of the **gospel of peace**; besides all these, taking the **shield of faith**, with which you can quench all the flaming darts of the evil one. And take the **helmet of salvation**, and the **sword of the Spirit**, which is the word of God. Pray at all times in the Spirit. (Eph. 6:10–18)

Will of God

You shall walk in all the way which the Lord your God has commanded you, that you may live, and that it may go well with you, and that you may live long in the land which you shall possess. (Deut. 5:33)

Jesus said to them, My food is to do the **will of Him** who sent Me, and to accomplish His work. (John 4:34)

I can do nothing on my own authority; as I hear, I judge; and my judgment is just, because I seek not my own will but the **will of Him** who sent me. (John 5:30)

For I have come down from heaven, not to do My own will, but the **will of Him** who sent me; and this is the **will of Him** who sent Me, that I should lose nothing of all that He has given Me, but raise it up at the last day. For this is the **will of my Father**, that every one who sees the Son and believes in Him should have eternal life; and I will raise him up at the last day. (John 6:38–40)

I appeal to you therefore, brethren, by the mercies of God, to present your bodies as a living sacrifice, holy and acceptable to God, which is your spiritual worship. Do not be conformed to this world but be transformed by the renewal of our mind, that you may prove what is the **will of God**, what is good and acceptable and perfect. (Rom. 12:1–2)

Therefore do not be foolish, but understand what the **will of the Lord** is. And do not get drunk with wine, for that is debauchery; but be filled with the Spirit. (Eph. 5:17–18)

For this is the **will of God**, your sanctification. (1 Thess. 4:3)

Rejoice always, pray constantly, give thanks in all circumstances; for this is the **will of God** in Christ Jesus for you. (1 Thess. 5:16–18)

Then I said, Lo, I have come to do **Thy will**, O God, as it is written of Me in the roll of the book. Then he added, Lo, I have come to do **Thy will**. (Heb. 10:7, 9)

For you have need of endurance, so that you may do the **will of God** and receive what is promised. (Heb. 10:36)

Now may the God of peace who brought again from the dead our Lord Jesus, the great shepherd of the sheep, by the blood of the eternal covenant, equip you with everything good that you may do **His will,** working in you that which is pleasing in His sight. (Heb. 13:20–21)

Of His **own will** He brought us forth by the word of truth that we should be a kind of first fruits of His creatures. (James 1:18)

For it is **God's will** that by doing right you should put to silence the ignorance of foolish men. (1 Pet. 2:15)

And this is the confidence which we have in Him, that if we ask anything according to **His will** He hears us. (1 John 5:14)

For Thou didst create all things, and by **Thy will** they existed and were created. (Rev. 4:11)

Winds

And behold, after them sprouted seven ears, thin and blighted by the **east wind**. (Gen. 41:6)

And the Lord turned a very strong **west wind**, which lifted the locusts and drove them into the Red Sea. (Exod. 10:19)

Then Moses stretched out his hand over the sea; and the Lord drove the sea back by a strong **east wind** all night. (Exod. 14:21)

Thou didst blow with thy **wind**, the sea covered them. (Exod. 15:10)

And there went forth a **wind** from the Lord, and it brought quails from the sea. (Num. 11:31)

The **east wind** lifts him up and he is gone; it sweeps him out of his place. (Job 27:21)

You whose garments are hot when the earth is still because of the **south wind**? And now men cannot look on the light when it is bright in the skies, when the **wind** has passed and cleared them. (Job. 37:17, 21)

What is the way to the place where the light is distributed, or where the **east wind is** scattered upon the earth? (Job. 38:24)

Who has ascended to heaven and come down? Who has gathered the **wind** in his fists? (Prov. 30:4)

Awake, O **north wind**, and come, O **south wind!** Blow upon my garden. (Sol. 4:16)

Then He said to me, Prophesy to the breath, prophesy, son of man, and say to the breath, thus says the Lord God: Come from the **four winds**, O breath, and breathe upon these slain, that they may live. (Ezek. 37:9)

Though he may flourish as the reed plant, the **east wind**, the **wind** of the Lord, shall come, rising from the wilderness; and his fountain shall dry up, his spring shall be parched. (Hosea 13:15)

After this I saw four angels standing at the four corners of the earth, holding back the **four winds** of the earth, that no **wind** might blow on earth or sea or against any tree. (Rev. 7:1)

Wisdom

Keep them and do them; for that will be your **wisdom** and your understanding in the sight of the peoples. (Deut. 4:6)

You shall be careful to do therefore as the Lord your God has commanded you; you shall not turn aside to the right hand or to the left. (Deut. 5:32)

Everything that I command you, you shall be careful to do; you shall not add to it or take from it. (Deut. 12:32)

And it shall be with him, and he shall read in it all the days of his life, that he may learn to fear the Lord his God, by keeping all the words of this law and these statutes, and doing them; that his heart may not be lifted up above his brethren, and that he may not turn aside from the commandment, either to the right hand or to the left. (Deut. 17:19–20)

The secret things belong to the Lord our God; but the things that are revealed belong to us and to our children for ever. (Deut. 29:29)

Give Thy servant therefore an **understanding mind** to govern Thy people, that I may **discern** between good and evil; behold, I now do according to your word. Behold, I give you a **wise** and **discerning mind**, so that none like you has been before you and none like you shall arise after you. (1 Kings 3:9, 12)

"With God" are **wisdom** and might; He has counsel and understanding. (Job 12:13)

The mouth of the righteous utters **wisdom**, and his tongue speaks justice. (Ps. 37:30)

Behold, Thou desirest truth in the inward being; therefore teach me **wisdom** in my secret heart. (Ps. 51:6)

So teach us to number our days that we may get a heart of **wisdom**. (Ps. 90:12)

Happy is the man who finds **wisdom**, and the man who gets understanding, for the gain from it is better than gain from silver and its profit better than gold. My son, keep sound

wisdom and discretion; let them not escape from your sight. (Prov. 3:13–14, 21)

He who is faithful in a very little is faithful also in much. (Luke 16:10)

Yet among the mature we do impart **wisdom** although it is not a **wisdom** of this age or of the rulers of this age, But we impart a secret and hidden **wisdom** of God, which God decreed before the ages for our glorification. (1 Cor. 2:6–7)

That the God of our Lord Jesus Christ, the Father of glory, may give you a spirit of **wisdom** and of revelation in the knowledge of Him, having the eyes of your hearts enlightened, that you may know what is the hope to which He has called you, what are the riches of His glorious inheritance in the saints, and what is the immeasurable greatness of His power in us who believe. (Eph. 1:17–19)

Do not quench the Spirit, do not despise prophesying, but **test everything**; hold fast what is good, abstain from every form of evil. (1 Thess. 5:19–22)

If any of you lacks **wisdom** let him ask God, who gives to all men generously and without reproaching. (James 1:5)

Know this, my beloved brethren. Let every man be quick to hear, slow to speak, slow to anger, for the anger of man does not work the righteousness of God. (James 1:19)

But the **wisdom** from above is first pure, then peaceable, gentle, open to reason, full of mercy and good fruits, without uncertainty or insincerity. (James 3:17)

This calls for **wisdom**: let him who has understanding reckon the number of the beast. (Rev. 18:18)

Word of God

You shall not add to the **word** which I command you, nor take from it. (Deut. 4:2)

But that man lives by every thing that proceeds out of the mouth of the Lord. (Deut. 8:3b)

But the **word** is very near you; it is in your mouth and in your heart. (Deut. 30:14)

So shall My **word** be that goes forth from My mouth; it shall not return to Me empty, but it shall accomplish that which I purpose, and prosper in the thing for which I sent it. (Isa. 55:11)

He sent forth His **word**, and healed them. (Ps. 107:20)

Forever, O Lord, Thy **word** is firmly fixed in the heavens. (Ps. 119:89)

But He answered, It is written, Man shall not live by bread alone, but by every **word** that proceeds from the mouth of God. (Matt. 4:4)

Heaven and earth will pass away, but My **words** will not pass away. (Matt. 24:35)

For with God nothing will be impossible. (Luke 1:37)

In the beginning was the **Word**, and the **Word** was with God, and the **Word** was God. (John 1:1)

For the **word of God** is living and active, sharper than any two-edge sword, piercing to the division of soul and spirit, of joints and marrow, and discerning the thoughts and intentions of the heart. (Heb. 4:12)

By faith, we understand that the world was created by the **word of God**, so that what is seen was made out of things which do not appear. (Heb. 11:3)

But the **word** of the Lord abides forever. (1 Pet. 1:25)

He is clad in a robe dipped in blood, and the name by which He is called is **The Word of God**. (Rev. 19:13)

Worship

And they shall stand every morning, **thanking** and **praising** the Lord, and likewise at evening. (1 Chron. 23:30)

The whole assembly **worshiped**, and the singers sang, and the trumpeters sounded. (2 Chron. 29:28)

Ascribe to the Lord the glory of His name; **worship** the Lord in holy array. (Ps. 29:2)

O come, let us **sing** to the Lord; let us make **joyful noise** to the rock of our salvation! Let us come into His presence with thanksgiving; let us make a **joyful noise** to Him with songs of **praise**! For the Lord is a great God, and a great King above all gods. O come, let us **worship** and bow down, let us **kneel** before the Lord, our Maker! For He is our God, and we are the people of His pasture, and the sheep of His hand. (Ps. 95:1–3, 6–7)

Worship the Lord in holy array; tremble before Him all the earth! (Ps. 96:9)

She did not depart from the temple, **worshiping** with fasting and prayer night and day. (Luke 2:37)

To present your bodies as a living sacrifice, holy and acceptable to God, which is your spiritual **worship**. (Rom. 12:1)

Therefore let us be grateful for receiving a kingdom that cannot be shaken, and thus let us offer to God acceptable **worship** with reverence and awe. (Heb. 12:28)

Who shall not fear and glorify Thy name, O Lord? For Thou alone art holy. All nations shall come and **worship** Thee. (Rev. 15:4)

Notes

About the Author

Dolly is a wife, mother of four, and grandmother of ten. She has resided in historic Pawling, New York, most of her life, which is famous for the Foundation for Christian Living, founded by Dr. Norman Vincent Peale and his wife; the John Kane House, a place where George Washington had his headquarters during the Revolutionary War; the home of James Earle Jones, famous actor; Lowell Thomas, pioneer radio broadcaster and famous world traveler; and Edward R. Murrow, American broadcast journalist and war correspondent.

She has attended Full Gospel Center, a Christian nondenominational church in LaGrangeville, New York, since 1983, which has shaped a major part of her Christian journey. She is currently retired and enjoying her family. She enjoys many hobbies: writing books and poems, cake decorating, music, photography, jewelry making, genealogy, reading, gardening, and scrapbooking. She has previously written a poem "The Twin Towers" (2014, Library of Congress).

Printed in the USA
CPSIA information can be obtained
at www.ICGtesting.com
LVHW041339310124
770461LV00072B/2128